ADVENTU

TIM KREITER

Published by Casa de Snapdragon LLC
Albuquerque, New Mexico, USA

Copyright © 2011 Tim Kreiter. All rights reserved.
Cover image and illustrations copyright © Tim Kreiter, all rights reserved.

No portion of this publication may be reproduced, stored in a retrieval system, or transmitted in any form or by any means, electronic, mechanical, photocopying, recording, or otherwise without the prior written permission of Tim Kreiter unless such copying is expressly permitted by federal copyright law. Address inquiries to Permissions, Casa de Snapdragon Publishing LLC, 12901 Bryce Avenue NE, Albuquerque, NM 87112.

The characters and actions in this book are real, only the names have been changed to protect the guilty.

Library of Congress Cataloging-in-Publication Data

Kreiter, Tim.
  Adventures of a substitute teacher / Tim Kreiter.
    p. cm.
  ISBN 978-0-9845681-7-8 (pbk.)
  1. Substitute teaching--Humor. I. Title.
  LB2844.1.S8K74 2011
  371.14'122--dc23
                            2011023147

Published by
Casa de Snapdragon Publishing LLC
12901 Bryce Avenue, NE
Albuquerque, NM 87112
http://www.casadesnapdragon.com
20110625

Printed in the United States of America

FOREWORD

On November 2, 2007, I retired from my 33-year career as an aerospace engineer at the Johnson Space Center. Some retirees go fishing, travel the world, or play golf. In December 2007, I chose to become a substitute teacher in the local public schools.

I dedicate this book to teachers everywhere. They report every day to class, prepare lesson plans, deal with kids of all temperaments, deal with parents of all temperaments, deal with school administrators of all temperaments, take work home, buy supplies with their own money, grade papers on weekends (and into the wee hours of the night), and shoulder the gargantuan responsibility of preparing America's kids for the future. God bless them!

Decades ago, entertainer Art Linkletter created a TV show entitled, "Kids Say the Darnedest Things." They still do - ask any teacher (or substitute). I have kept a diary of my experiences as a substitute and have shared it with my closest friends. They thought the stories were pretty funny and entreated me with "You ought to write a book." (I wonder how many wannabe writers have heard that line before?) I hope you will find my experiences funny too.

Substitute teachers rely on regular teachers to provide them with comprehensive lesson plans. Having a good lesson plan makes life a lot easier for us subs. But sometimes, due to an unforeseen emergency, teachers are unable to provide them, and subs are on their own. A good sub, like a Boy Scout, must always be prepared for such occasions and bring along backup plans and supplies.

When my four children were young, I read them a book entitled, "Gus, the Friendly Ghost." Gus lived in the rafters of old houses and rattled pots, pans, and lengths of chain to scare the human occupants. When he changed dwellings, he took his "bang-clank" equipment along with him. I affectionately refer to my backup teaching plans and supplies as my "bang-clank" equipment.

Mary Poppins carried a carpet bag full of her essential "nanny items." Lacking a good carpet bag, I selected a two foot by three foot zippered art satchel, and labeled it "my Texas briefcase." It was perfect for carrying my "bang-clank" equipment into the classroom. Wonder Woman had her lasso, Zorro had his sword, Indiana Jones had his bullwhip, and I had my briefcase.

The chapters are in chronological order, the stories are true, and the names have been changed to protect the guilty.

January 1, 2009

Contents

Foreword i
1. El Substituto 1
2. Artful Dodgers 4
3. MP3's on Mars 8
4. Mongol Hordes 11
5. The Businessman 14
6. Shark Farm 17
7. Oceanopoly 20
8. Tips for Teens 23
9. Sheer Magnetism 26
10. Pokin' a Pig 29
11. Thoughtless 32
12. Safety Moment 35
13. Draw Me 38
14. Dancing with the Stars 41
15. Incomplete Pass 44
16. Me, Me, Meat 47
17. Pizza Mania 49
18. Scarred for Life 52
19. Worth a Thousand Words 55
20. Wonder Woman to the Rescue 58
21. Toilet Flush Tag 61
22. Mouse in the House 64
23. Ambience 67
24. Excuses, Excuses 70
25. The Purple Circle 73
26. Tour of the Universe 77
27. Gumming Up the Works 80
28. Where Angels Fear to Tread 83
29. Sofa, Sofa, Who's Got the Sofa? 88
30. Beware of the Double Whammy 92
31. Rats and Rights 95
32. Strike Up the Band 98
33. Advice: Avoid Advisories 102
34. Plotting Paths 105
35. Unfathomable Levels of Laziness 108
36. Talent, Motivation, Attitude 111
37. Kiddie Kingdom 114
38. Double Helix Delight 118
39. Bonnie's Band 122
40. Promises, Promises 126

41. Potties, Potties	130
42. Marshmallow Toes	133
43. Beach Therapy	136
44. Things Failed to Add Up	140
45. Bubble Gum Bribe	144
46. Sanitized Ears	148
47. Author, Author	151
48. Red Carpet Event	155
49. Movin' and Groovin'	159
50. Skunk Attack	163
About the Author	166

CHAPTER 1

El Substituto

Several decades ago, Hollywood made a movie about teachers. In that movie the school secretary, in search for a substitute teacher, misdialed a phone number and reached an inmate at the local mental facility. "Would you please report to Hollywood High tomorrow morning and teach American history?" she asked. Being a mental patient and being accustomed to the absurd, he replied, "Of course!" The next morning, he walked into class dressed as Abraham Lincoln. The kids were giggling at first, but quieted down immediately when he began reading the

Gettysburg address with all the authority and dignity of old Abe himself. No substitute could have made a more positive impact on the class than the Abe impersonator from Quiet Hills Mental Hospital.

Rustic Ranch administrators require that substitute applicants have a college degree, pass a background check, and complete training (most of which is of the computer-based, interactive variety) to qualify them for classroom assignments. The Rustic Ranch school district employs an automated computer program for contacting its substitutes, thus ensuring that only certified substitutes are called and never the certifiably insane. (Sorry, Abe.)

During the substitute teacher orientation session held December 2007, applicants were asked to designate on their registration forms what type of assignments they preferred. Having spent my career as an aerospace engineer, I naturally wrote down Math, Trigonometry, Algebra, Science, Astronomy, and Physics.

At 5:55 A.M. the next morning I received a call from the RR Schools, asking me to teach Spanish. To me, this sounded absurd, since the only Spanish words I knew were: *Buenos dias, gracias,* and *vaya con Dios.* But, with all the gusto of the Abe impersonator, I gave it a try.

I reported for my very first assignment dressed as a Gringo. I wrote my name in large black letters at the top of the white board. Underneath I printed, "El Substituto." Thankfully the regular teacher, who spoke Spanish fluently, had left me very specific lesson plans. Students were to complete exercises from their Spanish workbooks; I merely needed to keep the class focused. (The use of the word "merely" suggests that keeping classes focused is an easy task. Ha! In the ensuing months I would gain a new respect for teachers who maintained order and discipline in their classrooms.)

A smile and a sense of humor go a long way when you are leading a class of 30 or more teens. I discovered that kids needed to obtain my permission to make a trip to the restroom. Wow! Did I have power or what? My policy, established that very first day, was to always allow a student to use the restroom. I have never regretted that decision.

I wondered how frequently I would be asked to substitute. The next day at 5:55 A.M. I received another call. Visions of quadratic formulas danced in my head as I picked up the receiver. Imagine my surprise when they asked me to teach preschoolers at the Sparkling Stars Preschool!

When I reported for duty at Sparkling Stars Preschool, I was relieved to discover that I had a co-teacher helper. She was the regular teacher's aide and knew the daily routine. The younger the student, the more important it is to adhere to a schedule. The preschoolers had a very well defined schedule and the kids, even though they were only 4 or 5 years old, knew it precisely. There was snack time, potty break time, playground time, story time, and nap time.

Little children are very accepting and trusting. The kids warmed up to me quickly and, before I knew it, I was reading them stories and drawing pictures with them. I envisioned myself as their grandpa and the day went well.

At playground time, we bundled them up against the cold and headed for the swing sets. The key thing during playground time is to count heads going and make sure it equals the head count coming back.

One cute thing happened on the playground. Perhaps I noticed it because I was a rocket scientist in a previous existence. One of the playground toys was a stubby rocket ship mounted on a sturdy, or so it seemed, coil spring. One of our little boys, who was very overweight, hopped on the rocket and set it into motion. It promptly nose-dived into the cold turf - a very bad situation for rockets of any kind! A class mate noticed the predicament, scurried over, and hopped on the back of the rocket. From then on, the space faring duo experienced straight and level flight - AOK!

The technical assignments continued to elude me. Rustic Ranch needed a substitute for first grade. On this occasion, I had no aids. It was me against the world! A world of first graders. But they saw the gray hair, the kind (and gullible) eyes, and the day went well. The question of my age came up and I made a contest out of it. I asked each child to guess my age and to write the number on an index card. They were to fold the card and pass it to the front of the room. On the first card I opened, the child had written "16." I twitched my eyebrows a few times, flexed my biceps, and shouted, "Yes!" Then I opened the second card. It read, "120." That brought this rocket scientist auguring back to earth.

Fourteen guessed me to be younger and four guessed me to be older than my actual age. One was within 2 years (just lucky). I told this story to the adult choir members at my church and one charitable individual suggested that I had read the sixteen upside down.

I had a cartooning lesson in my Texas brief case full of bang-clank equipment, so I taught the kids how to draw simple cartoons. At the end of the day, two little girls wrote a note of thanks on their cartoons, handed them to me, hugged me, and said, "You were a great teacher." Hugs and words of appreciation are the real paychecks for teachers (and substitutes) of all ages.

CHAPTER 2

Artful Dodgers

When I attended high school back in the '50s, movies were a novelty in the classroom and students really appreciated the diversion. We used 16 millimeter film projectors and projection screens. The school even had a projection club for training projectionists. It was an honor to be called upon to show a film to schoolmates.

The only movie I remember seeing those many years ago was entitled "The Lady or the Tiger?" Either that was the only film in our library or the others were truly unremarkable. It was a romantic tale about a powerful queen and her two-timing boyfriend. The queen discovered that

Lord Henry was seeing the voluptuous Lady Marion on the side. The queen was furious and placed Lord Henry in an arena. There were two doors. Behind one was Lady Marion and behind the other was a very hungry Bengal tiger. Lord Henry gave the Queen a pathetic, "help me" look. The Queen smiled slyly and pointed to the door on the right. As Henry reached to open the door on the right, the screen went blank and words appeared: "Will it be the Lady or the tiger?" The teacher turned on the lights and asked us to write a theme about the story ending.

Celluloid film and mechanical projectors have disappeared from the public schools. Today, classrooms have video monitors and video libraries containing scores, if not hundreds, of educational movies. Teachers insert a DVD (digital video disc) into a slot, press the play button, and Shazam! - a color movie.

I accepted an assignment to teach science at the middle school (eighth and ninth graders).

At last, I thought, a subject near and dear to my heart. When I reported for duty, I was informed that the regular teacher was conducting a science fair in the auditorium and those students who had prepared exhibits would be absent from class. My orders were to show a video to the remaining students.

Right away it was obvious to me that the two dozen or so students who came to class that day were non-scientist types. When I was a student, movie time was special. It still is special, but in a different way. Students use the occasion to sit where they please and to gossip with one another during the movie. The teacher left the following instructions, which I dutifully announced prior to pressing the play button: "Write down ten new concepts you learned from the film."

My home town had a theater named "The Ritz" - a very inappropriate name for a variety of reasons. The proprietor, a perpetually frowning man named Barry Lacosta, used to pace up and down the aisles during the movie shouting, "You kids pipe down!" My role in that science class was similar to Barry Lacosta's. One young guy was particularly disruptive, and it appeared to me that he had developed the obnoxious side of his personality to perfection. I quietly went to him and politely invited him to come with me and take the nice seat by my desk. Reluctantly he complied.

When the bell rang (to everyone's relief, especially mine) the boy smiled and shouted to the class that I was the best substitute he ever had. All the rest of the substitutes had yelled at him and the last substitute had "written him up" 3 times and ejected him from class. Could that last sub have been Barry Lacosta?

Biology is a science, so I felt reasonably comfortable accepting an assignment at the high school to cover for the Biology teacher. He had a full time associate and she was present that morning and was familiar with the routine. I became her assistant and distributed worksheets and shared duties. We team-taught two separate classes that morning and students completed Biology worksheets during class. They were all juniors and seniors and much more focused than the eighth and ninth grade "scientists" I had previously taught.

When I took Biology in high school, the teacher was the football coach. He was a no-nonsense guy who, on occasion, would recruit husky male Biology students for his football team. The Biology teacher I was substituting for at the Rustic Ranch High School was the wrestling coach. He was absent that day because he had taken the varsity team to a wrestling tournament. A handful of husky male Biology students were absent from class as well.

After I finished my morning duties as a Biology teacher, I reported to the gym to lead the junior varsity wrestlers. I had no idea what was coming. A dozen or so energetic teens bounced into the dressing room. They all had dyed their hair orange. Orange hair was the trademark of the wrestlers that year. One black student retained his natural hair color and I couldn't resist teasing him to "get with the program." He smiled politely, as if he had heard that one before.

The group dressed in their sweat suits and piled onto a giant air mattress in the corner of the room, where they began slugging each other, strangling each other, and rolling all over the mattress. The scene reminded me of a litter of lion clubs pummeling one another in their den. I carry a whistle for such occasions and I gave it a piercing screech. All the orange heads simultaneously rotated in my direction. I gave them their orders: "Jog around the track for twenty minutes, then play dodge ball."

Jogging has never been a popular teen activity. When I played football, the coach used it as punishment. If you were late for practice, you had to jog once around the track. Sass the coach and you jogged five times around. The wrestlers, now lacking the energy they had just demonstrated on the mattress, plodded to the second floor track and commenced jogging. As the minutes ticked by, it seemed like a third of the junior varsity joggers disappeared to parts unknown. When we reassembled to play dodge ball they magically reappeared.

The dodge ball exercise was a frightening and potentially deadly experience. Their gusto suddenly returned as they prepared for the kill. They grabbed volleyballs and raced into a large, padded room. Then all you-know-what broke loose! I was truly amazed at the speed with which they threw the volleyballs. All of them appeared to have major league pitching arms. It wouldn't have surprised me if ball speeds reached 90 miles per hour. When a ball hit a padded wall, it made an earth shattering cannon smack and left a circular dent. When it hit one of the boys, it knocked him off his feet. I peered cautiously from the doorway and never entered the deadly arena. Fortunately, there were no fatalities on my watch!

After the brutal, welting, dodge ball session ceased, they all filed back into the dressing room. I looked at the clock and, to my dismay, there were still 30 more minutes to go. I noticed that there was a large whiteboard above the mattress, so I thought I'd give the team a cartooning lesson.

I proceeded to show them how to draw the balloon head and the gesture action or "stick figure." When I finished, I invited them to come to the whiteboard and create their own drawings. That was a mistake. They spent the remainder of the period drawing obscene cartoons. I went home certain of two things: 1) a little bit of knowledge is a dangerous thing and 2) do not caste your pearls before the swine.

Chapter 3

MP3's on Mars

When school resumed after the Christmas holidays, students showed up in class with their own "bang clank" equipment - palm pilots, MP3 players, cell phones that text, etc. School administrators forbid students to use electronic devices in class, but the students are crafty. They wear hooded sweatshirts and/or stocking caps to conceal the earphones, and they string connecting wires under their shirts and blouses. Every student today has the know-how to be an undercover spy for a federal agency. What I faced after Christmas was a battle for attention - involving student "bang clank" equipment.

On a frosty morning in January, I was called upon to teach an astronomy lesson to a middle high science class. After getting permission from the regular teacher, I dug deep into my Texas brief case and produced a CD containing a PowerPoint presentation of the best pictures taken by the Mars orbiter and the Mars Rover. These pictures are "anaglyphs," (i.e., stereo pairs that give the illusion of three dimensions when viewed with red and blue glasses.) I just happened to have three dozen red and blue glasses among my "bang clank" equipment.

"Hoods off and earphones out," I announced as I distributed the anaglyph glasses. I also asked the students to treat the glasses with special care, as I intended to use them in the future: "No bending, twisting, chewing on, or mutilating, please!" The class seemed to enjoy the show, and moved their heads from side to side to enhance the stereo effects. Seeing a classroom full of kids wearing stereo glasses and bobbing their heads is a sight to behold. After the show, they bombarded me with questions about Mars. *Is there water on Mars? What is the gravity of Mars? Is there any air to breathe on Mars? When will we send men and women to Mars?*

I prophesied that scientists and explorers of their generation may be the astronauts who explore the red planet. I can just see them making footprints in the red dust while they listen to their 21st Century electronic devices, which they smuggled into their helmets and space suits.

The Rustic Ranch high school divides the school day into blocks. Each block lasts an hour and forty-five minutes. I don't know how the regular teachers keep the students occupied for an entire block, but they do. When a substitute takes over, the lesson material never seems to last long enough, and the sub often has 30 minutes left over. In the broadcasting industry that is known as dead air time.

A dead air time situation occurred while I was teaching a Biology class. Earlier that month, I watched an educational program about the world's ten most intriguing, unsolved mysteries. I developed a family feud game around that topic and added it to my "bang clank" equipment. This is what I selected to fill the dead air time in the biology class. We divided the class into three families and each family made up a list of what unsolved mysteries they thought may have made the top ten.

When they had finished making their lists, we compiled point totals for Families A, B, and C. The winning family members got treats - the little candy lozenges called "Smarties." The losing family members got the small lollipops known as "Dum Dums." The dead air space was filled and the students had fun.

To complete the learning experience, the entire class brainstormed how to solve some of these mysteries using the scientific method, which they had studied earlier in the year. Who knows, at some future date, graduates of Rustic Ranch High School may unlock the mysteries of the

Loch Ness monster, the pyramids, Stonehenge, the Bermuda Triangle, Atlantis, flying saucers, near-death experiences, Area 51 in Nevada, psychic phenomena, ghosts, crop circles, and spontaneous combustion of humans. They may even establish contact with alien civilizations.

It could happen!

CHAPTER 4

Mongol Hordes

When George Washington was 14 years old, he wrote 110 "Rules of Civility and Decent Behavior." The object of the book was to "polish manners, keep alive the best affections of the heart, impress the obligation of moral virtues, teach how to treat others in social relations, and, above all, inculcate the practice of a perfect self-control."

Rule number one offers this advice: "Every action done in company ought to be with some sign of respect to those that are present." Rule 10: "When you sit down, keep your feet firm and even, without putting one on the other or crossing them." Rule 14: "Turn not your back to others especially in speaking; jog not the table or desk on which another reads or writes; lean not upon any one." Rule 24: "Do not laugh too much or too loud in public." Rule 49: "Use no reproachful language against anyone; neither curse nor revile." Rule 70: "Reprehend not the imperfections of others, for that belongs to parents, masters, and superiors."

Legend has it that a certain prison distributed a joke book to inmates. Jokes were numbered 1 through 300. The prisoners had memorized the jokes to the extent that they only had to repeat the number to appreciate the joke. As one of the rituals after the evening meal, someone would stand and voice a number, e.g., "21!" The crowd would roar! One day a new prisoner joined the ranks, received a copy of the joke book, and set about to memorize the contents. Wishing to gain favor with his peers he stood up after the meal and shouted, "36!" Silence. He tried again, "73!" Silence. He had heard others repeat "21," so he boldly bellowed, "21!" Silence. He dejectedly sat down and asked the prisoner seated next to him, "Why didn't they laugh?" The man replied "Some people can tell jokes and some can't."

In a perfect world, we'd ask students to memorize Washington's "Rules of Civility and Decent Behavior," and when they broke a rule, we would call out a number, e.g., "10!" They would immediately respond by planting their feet firmly on the floor, readjusting their posture, and focusing on the task at hand. Ha!

During an assignment at a middle school (6th and 7th graders), the rules of civility and decent behavior broke down to the point that a teacher in an adjacent room came through the door to complain about the noise. She informed my class that they were so noisy that her class was unable to concentrate on their lessons. Silently I thought, "I'll trade you classes!" Audibly, I apologized to the teacher for my failure to maintain control.

After the irate teacher left the room I turned to the temporarily quiet Mongol hoard and spoke man-to-man with them. "You had all better hunker down and study and take your education seriously, or you'll all end up as bums on the street!" I shared the story with my brother, and he suggested that I take a bugle to class and sound "RECALL" when noisy situations arose. I did clip a police whistle to my badge lanyard and it comes in handy when students violate Rule 24.

That same day, I noticed that yesterday's sub had left a note for the teacher saying that the period 7 and 8 classes were especially troublesome. Forewarned, I put on my Frankenstein monster frown as they took their seats and made grave threats to those who misbehaved. Surprisingly, the class time went well. Meanness works.

There were a few "wise guys" that required special attention. One little guy couldn't sit still. He'd roam all over the room, checking on fellow classmates. Finally, I asked him, "Richard, are there more than one of you?" (I could have asked him if he were ubiquitous, but that would have just produced 30 dumb looks.) The class laughed at that query. A classmate added, "He always does that."

An adage seemed appropriate that afternoon, so I pontificated: "Humans behave in one of three ways. There are the wise who learn from others' mistakes; there are those with common sense who learn from their own mistakes (and never repeat their mistakes); and there are foolish people, who make the same mistake over and over and never learn anything." Richard immediately replied, "That's me! That's me!"

During the final fifteen minutes of class, I read two stories to these exuberant 7th graders, namely, "The Insolent Boy" and "Beware of the First Drink," both taken from McGuffey's Third Eclectic Reader. When I finished, a young lad in the first row tossed out a compliment: "You must be very intelligent! Are you a genius or something?" I couldn't tell if he was serious or was trying to blow smoke until the bell rang. The perfect response, which I didn't think of at the time, would have been, "I'm smarter than the average bear!" (But these little whiskers have never seen the old TV cartoon series, "Yogi Bear.")

I felt good at the end of the day, because the period 7 and 8 classes had at least honored George Washington's Rule 1: "Every action done in company ought to be with some sign of respect to those that are present."

Chapter 5

The Businessman

The expression I use to describe impossibly busy situations is, "This is like putting socks on an octopus." I uttered my impossibility mantra a dozen times the day I accepted an assignment to teach second graders at the Rustic Ranch elementary school. Second graders are incredibly observant, vocal, and savvy on what is and what is not fair. In addition, most are thin skinned and could hear a pin drop in a bowling alley.

It was a chilly February morning and the children arrived in big furry coats, stocking hats, and mittens. As one little girl peeled off her red furry hooded coat, I did a double take! She was, as the saying goes, the "spittin' image" of my wife when she was seven or eight years old. It brought a tear to my eye. Have you ever wished you could pop into a time machine and travel back into the past to observe your favorite person as a child? I felt like I had been granted that privilege.

When you substitute for a regular teacher in an elementary school, you have BIG shoes to fill. Elementary school teachers have to establish an intricate network of rules and procedures to cover every imaginable classroom situation. They are called to do the impossible. The writers of the Constitution could well have been elementary school teachers.

As I scanned the classroom I noticed coffee cans containing clothes pins. Each pin had a student's name printed on it. There were clipboards hanging in strategic places bristling with spreadsheets. There were envelopes on the door, held in place by sturdy magnets. Activity centers, labeled and color-coded, occupied the corners of the room. Giant shelves had been provided to hold the students' clothing and back packs, and each student was assigned a bin (and heaven help them if they put their belongings in another person's bin).

For most sub assignments, a lesson plan on a sheet of 8-1/2 by 11 inch paper is adequate for the day. When asked to teach second graders, however, you need a DVD providing hour by hour instructions. Chapter 1: Collecting lunch money and sending it to the cafeteria; Chapter 2: Taking roll and checking seat assignments; Chapter 3: The morning trip to the library; Chapter 4: Recess protocol; Chapter 5: Timeline of study topics (math, story time, penmanship, etc.); Chapter 6: Settling disputes; Chapter 7: Clean up guidelines; Chapter 8: Use of tools (clothes pins, clipboards, treat jar, etc); and so forth. Does this sound like putting socks on an octopus or what?

My primary directive was to teach the second graders math, reading, and spelling, however, I discovered that the great tapestry of learning was laced with threads of innumerable iridescent interruptions.

For example, a little girl came to me and said, "Jared is staring at me!" (I said, "Jared, stop staring at Lexie!") Another teary-eyed little fellow said, "Quentin is calling me names!" ("Quentin, stop calling him names!")

One little guy was the self-appointed class cop. He quietly came to me and said, "The class is being too noisy and I can't concentrate!" ("Alright class, quiet down!") Later in the day, I sat Bircher in the corner for disrupting the class. The "cop" led me to a clipboard on the wall and said that it was SOP to have Bircher sign and date the form to document the offense. (Bircher refused!) I didn't press it. There were larger fish to fry that day.

I noticed Aaron really concentrating on what appeared to be an extracurricular activity. I looked closer and saw that he was creating a spreadsheet on a piece of notebook paper. On it he wrote his classmates' names and other cryptic information. Students visited him throughout the day and he scribbled information on his spreadsheet.

Even though I was busy putting socks on the octopus, I managed to sandwich myself in between his regular customers to ask, "Aaron, what are you doing?" He replied, "I'm working on my business." My business? Do entrepreneurs start in second grade? Was this Amway? Is he (heaven forbid) a second grade drug dealer? An unsocked tentacle pulled me away from the interview and, before I knew it, the bell rang and the room cleared, leaving the question of the day unanswered.

When I got home, I shared the entrepreneur story with my wife and she immediately asked me the obvious, "What was his business?" She was really irritated that I didn't find out.

A few weeks later, I subbed at the same school and, on my lunch break, went to Aaron's classroom. I knocked and Miss Abacrombe, the regular teacher, came to the door. I informed her that I had been her sub a few weeks ago and there was an unanswered question that was bothering me, namely, "What was Aaron's business?" She gave me a puzzled look and said, "I have no idea. Let's ask Aaron."

The teacher asked Aaron to come to her desk and we asked the 64 dollar question.

He said that he made paper telephones and sold them to his classmates for erasers. The erasers are shaped like little rectangles with dollars bills printed on them. Both the teacher and I chuckled over Aaron's inventiveness. In a few years he will likely be taking in real dollars.

The following week I taught the Business class at high school. When I shared Aaron's story with them they were really impressed, and that in itself (impressing high school students) was impressive. World, make way for Aaron!

CHAPTER 6

Shark Farm

When I was in fourth grade (many decades ago) our school was too small to have a dedicated music teacher, so our regular teacher, Miss McMillan assumed those duties. Once a week, we shoved the chairs back to the walls, formed a circle in the middle of the room, and sang "The Farmer in the Dell."

You know the routine. The teacher picks a farmer to stand in the middle of the circle, usually her pet. Then, as the class sings and circles wonder boy, he picks a wife (always the class cutie with her headful of blonde curls). Cutie picks a child, and so on down through the animal kingdom. Although it was never meant to be a popularity contest, it was. As new kid on the block, I was always picked next to last as the "rat," and I picked the only remaining child (Charles K.) as the cheese. Every week, the routine was the same. Rats, rats, rats! Was I destined to crawl through life with no more dignity than Charlotte's friend, Pendleton?

Today's schools are a lot more sophisticated. They do have dedicated music teachers, and I was called to substitute for one at the Colonel Dexter North elementary school one chilly February morning. I tossed a music concentration game into my Texas brief case and grabbed my trumpet. Bang clank equipment takes on a new dimension when you're teaching music.

I taught K through 5. For the kindergarten and first grade children, the teacher had left instructions to listen to a CD of the classical opera, "The Farmer and His Animals." Although this stirred some not so good memories of farmers (especially those living in dells), I complied.

I spread butcher paper on the floor, distributed marking pens, and instructed them to draw pictures of the animals they heard on the CD. To my surprise and delight, they were good little artists. Each drew their favorite animals - hippos (how did they get on the farm?), cows, dogs, cats, bunnies, sheep, giraffes (who let them in?), and fish. I was relieved that no one chose to draw a rat! Ha!

I helped one child complete his picture of a chicken, and others noticed that I could draw. I immediately became the "Big Man on Campus." Everyone wanted me to draw an animal for them. My first commission was to draw a shark (must have been a land shark, because there are no oceans on a farm). Pretty soon everyone wanted me to draw them a shark. When the bell rang, the butcher paper looked like a "Jaws" movie poster. It appeared as if all the farm animals were the unfortunate victims of a shark feeding frenzy!

The teacher failed to leave lesson plans for the second and third grade classes, so I improvised. I had a concentration game about music symbols, and I had the kids sit on the floor around the pegboard while we played the game. The game was similar to the old TV game show, "Concentration."

After the game, I brought forth my silver trumpet and demonstrated how to play it. Now I must confess to you that I was a four year member of the Ohio State University Marching Band, and that I am an avid Buckeye. This particular elementary school was located a few states west of Ohio, so I was playing where Buckeyes feared to tread.

Nevertheless, I couldn't resist teaching them a song that the band played on special occasions, entitled, "Round on the End and High in the Middle." I wrote the words on the whiteboard and played the tune on the trumpet. When the bell rang, the second and third grade converts marched out of the room singing "Round on the Ends and High in the Middle." I felt pretty proud carrying the OSU gospel to a new generation in a foreign land!

A teacher in an adjacent classroom popped her head in the door to check out the racket. Apparently, the sound of the trumpet spilled over into her room. Was she a Wolverine from the University of Michigan? Was she going to ask me to play "Hail to the Conquering Heroes"? Or was she just seeking peace and quiet? (It was mostly the latter.)

My last challenge of the day was to direct the 5th grade choir. I soon discovered that this was easier said than done. Just lining them up on stage took half the class period. The regular teacher must have her hands full with this bunch. Another "putting socks on an octopus" situation.

The lesson plan called for us to rehearse songs from their new musical entitled (of all things) "Rats!" Finally, rats were getting some press! The music was on a CD, and after getting help from another member of the school staff, we finally got the CD player to work. That gobbled up another 20 minutes. Finally, I raised my baton and began.

In most crackerjack choirs and orchestras, the musicians actually make eye contact with the director. Fifth graders make ear contact. Their heads are usually turned 90 degrees as they chat with friends. We struggled to sing two songs from the musical before the bell rang. I think the regular teacher would have been proud of me.

I can sum up my opinion of directing 5th grade choirs in three words: Rats! Rats! Rats!

Chapter 7

Oceanopoly

In the movie, "Superman 2," three Kryptonian villains (General Zod and his two nasty companions) were accidentally released from their phantom zone prison, and they made a B-line for earth. In their search for Kal-El, they brought death and destruction to the people of earth. In one scene, Superman's arch enemy Lex Luthor met the three invincible tormentors, smiled, and exclaimed, "Ah! My kind of people!"

My avocation for the past 30 years has been creating educational games. My goal has been to make learning fun by capitalizing on the innate human traits of competitiveness and curiosity. The majority of my games have been used in the church to teach Biblical principles. On my logo appear the words, "Slipping Sneakers on the Scriptures." I have also developed games that were used in the workplace to teach participative management techniques, to develop interpersonal skills, to discover temperament type, and to cultivate institutional safety.

When I drew an assignment to teach the "Family School" classes at the Paradise Ridge Elementary School, I experienced the same thrilling moment that Lex Luthor did when he met the three kindred spirits from Krypton, because, to my delight, I discovered that students had created educational games about their science topic of the semester, namely oceanology. I smiled and sighed, "Ah! My kind of people!"

Family school students receive home schooling for half a day, then report to public school for the other half. Nine students attended the morning session and 11 came in the afternoon. We held classes in a portable building adjacent to the main facility. The environment was "homey" and the teacher-to-student ratio was ideal.

The lesson plan called for a show and tell, wherein each child showed his or her game to the class and explained the rules. After all of the games had been introduced, the students formed groups of three to six each and played the games. Every child's game was played during the period.

Each student had created a colorful and imaginative game with game board, directions, and accessories. Ginger made an Oceanopoly game, obviously patterned after Monopoly. Hey! Imitation is the sincerest form of flattery! Players moved their tokens (sea shells) to the various oceans and seas and, during their "aquatic" travels, answered trivia questions about sea creatures and environmental concerns.

Carlos patterned his game (Mystery in the Blue) after the popular board game, "Clue." Players had to guess 1) the name of the insensitive marine-life destroyer, 2) what poor defenseless sea creature had been eliminated, and 3) what weapon had caused its demise (spear, net, pollution, etc.).

Jennifer created Ocean Pictionary. Each OP player drew a card from the deck upon which was printed the name of an ocean dweller (whale, shark, sponge, starfish, coral, etc.). The player carefully shielded that card from view of other players, and then, using a dry erase pen and miniature whiteboard, drew their rendition of the creature named on the card. Kids had to guess what was being drawn. An egg timer was used to limit length of play.

Bethany created a game entitled "Oceans to Oceans," which was inspired by the game "Apples to Apples." The group playing Oceans to Oceans needed another player, so I sat down on the carpet and joined them. I had never played Apples to Apples, so the Oceans to Oceans author gave me some one-on-one tutoring. This was the most complicated of the four games, but fun to play.

The zipper of my Texas briefcase was silent that day, for to have reached for any of my bang-clank equipment would have been the equivalent of "bringing coals to Newcastle!"

CHAPTER 8

Tips for Teens

Hollywood produced a series of very popular movies in the 1940's about a gang of New York City delinquents known as "The Dead End Kids" a.k.a. "The East Side Kids" a.k.a. "The Bowery Boys." Leo Gorcey alias "Mugsey" was the gang leader and Huntz Hall alias "Sach" was the gang goof ball. A trademark scene was Mugsey slapping Sach over the head with his own ball cap for acting stupid. Actually, Mugsey slapped all the gang members around, because they were all stupid. Role modeling for teens had reached its nadir in the 40's.

One bleak Tuesday I was asked to teach ISS (In-School Suspension) classes at the Rustic Ranch mid high school. The ISS youngsters met in a portable building. When I stepped into the room, about a half dozen kids sized me up. I scanned the room to see if Mugsey and Sach were there. Fortunately, another seasoned teacher was present. Dispatchers always send policemen out in pairs for dangerous assignments. The same thing must apply to ISS classrooms.

One kid spent the whole day in an enclosed 4-foot by 4-foot cubical. All I saw was his back. Apparently, he was in solitary confinement! The only time he moved was at lunch time. The rest of the day he stared at worksheets on his desk. I don't think he had a pencil (some ISS kids must not be allowed to have sharp objects).

I overheard a conversation between two other kids. Kid 1: "While I was at a restaurant with my mom and dad last night, I spotted a twenty dollar bill on the cash register while we were checking out. When no one was looking, I blew real hard, and it fell to the floor. I picked it up and kept it. When we got home, my Mom spotted the cash and asked me where I got it. I told her that I found it in the restroom." Kid 2 contemplated for a moment before contributing to the "can you top this?" contest.

Kid 2: "When my Dad leaves a 5 dollar tip at a restaurant, I lag behind and snatch it off the table. If I see dollar bills on other empty tables, I scoop them up too on the way out." I thought, "Here's a kid that must be on every waitress's most wanted list." I imagine Al Capone and John Dillinger must have engaged in similar contests when they got together to swap stories.

As this discussion continued to degenerate into the dark abyss, the fire alarm sounded and we all filed out of the room. Ah, out of the dungeon and into the bright sunshine and blue skies! I stood by a third kid, whom I just met - hoping for an upbeat conversation.

Kid 3: "Wouldn't it be awesome if the school really burned down?"

Kid 4: "Hey! Somebody stole my wallet!" I glanced at Kid 1 and Kid 2 to see if I could detect any suspicious bulges in their pockets.

On another ISS assignment, I was responsible for about a dozen ISS students. They were supposed to be completing worksheets during the class period, but instead, they mulled around the room, like prisoners in a recreation yard. I distinctly felt that my role was that of a "Warden." Three girls escaped from class and one boy had his coat stolen on my watch. Next time they can find another warden. I seriously thought about adding handcuffs to my bang-clank equipment.

The following week I taught the "Core Math" class at high school. Core Math is for kids who have flunked previous math courses. After 15 minutes with them, I can understand why. I have never seen a group less interested in math. I thought the entire Core Math class was deaf when I called the role. As it turned out, they were just ignoring me.

According to the lesson plan, I was to stand up front and review a math worksheet with the Core Math students. Since I couldn't even hold their attention long enough to take attendance, I made a quick battlefield decision. Hoping they might listen to one of their own, I asked, "Would any of you care to teach this class today?" Surprisingly, a young girl named Nancy sitting in the front row raised her hand! I handed her the worksheet and dry erase marker, sat down, and said, "Go!"

Nancy did a fine job. She had better success than I would have had, and it gave her hands-on teaching experience. There were nonetheless a few notable distractors. Two kids (boy and girl) kept hugging one another during class. I asked them if they were married. They blushed and took separate seats. (They reconnected in the hall after the bell rang.)

A boy named Turner roamed around the room as Nancy was teaching the math. I asked him the standard roaming-around-the-room question, "Are there more than one of you?" Turner smiled and took his seat.

A girl named Sabrina defiantly ignored Nancy, me, and the math worksheet. She had pointed her desk 180 degrees away from Nancy, and she spent the entire period making obscene gestures to a boy in the back of the room (who may or may not have been awake). I asked Sabrina if she had eyes in the back of her head. Her response was a glare - thankfully no gestures.

Major league baseball teams have farm clubs for developing up and coming talent. I am convinced that the "Core Math" class is the farm club for ISS. Next time I do ISS, I'll check closely for some tell-tale "Core Math" worksheets on their desks.

CHAPTER 9

Sheer Magnetism

The Rustic Ranch mid high school contacted me shortly after spring break. They needed someone to teach physical science, in particular "magnetism," to eighth graders. There were 3 blocks or periods. A teaching aid would be present to help me in blocks 1 and 3, but I would be alone for block 2.

The regular teacher told me that she had some good kids in the block 1 and 3 classes, but she warned me to beware of the block 2 class. To quote her verbatim, "They will be a handful!" (She was right!)

When I was a kid, I had an electronic game called "Magnetic

Football." It featured a metal, vibrating electronic football field and 22 jittery, magnetic, miniature "players." There were 11 red team members and 11 yellow team members. One player (the designated ball carrier) had a little spring-loaded arm which held a tiny felt football and, supposedly, he could throw a pass. To complete the pass, the felt ball had to hit a teammate of the same color. This feat was the equivalent of shooting down a high-flying bat with a slingshot, blindfolded.

The object of Magnetic Football was to line up both teams - offense and defense - on the metal playing field; place the ball carrier (with the felt ball) behind his "blockers"; flip the switch to activate the playing field; then hope that the ball carrier reached the right goal line before being touched by an opposing player.

It was the most frustrating game I ever played, and I noticed this the first (and only) time I played it. Once the metal playing field began to vibrate, the players rattled all over the field with absolutely no order or intelligence. The ball carrier invariably jiggled in circles and usually headed for the wrong goal line - we called him "Wrong Way Riegels," after the University of California player who recovered a fumble in the 1929 Rose Bowl and ran toward the wrong goal.

Unlike the block 1 and 3 students who, upon entering the class room, took their seats, and appeared ready to learn, the block 2 kids entered the room in a frenzy, looking much like the magnetic football team players. Unfortunately, I had no switch to shut off the vibrating field so I had to resort to my whistle. Just getting them seated was a touchdown for me.

A boy named Mario was particularly rambunctious. I whipped out a piece of paper and shouted, "Mario, I'm putting your name on the list!" About a minute later, by pure coincidence, a security guard came in and asked, "Which one of you is Mario?" The guard escorted Mario out of class! I turned to the class and said, "Well, I guess I can remove Mario's name from the list." I was hoping they would think that I had a magnetic mental link with the security forces, and that the rest of them better stay on my good side.

The security guard returned three additional times during block 2 and extracted three more gremlins. The three extracted students had apparently committed offenses earlier in the day, and the security team hadn't tracked them down until block 2.

Two block 2 girls insisted on sitting upon one another's laps as they were completing their worksheets. In an attempt to embarrass them into taking separate seats, I asked them if they were Siamese Twins. Considering the subject was magnetism, I insisted, "Miss North Pole, please sit here; Miss South Pole, please sit there."

Charles, who sat in the back of the room with his arms folded over his chest, had a King-and-I hairdo (i.e., bald), and an aloof attitude. He refused to do his worksheet. It appeared to me that he'd been habitually boycotting worksheets in all of his classes for quite some time. I quietly approached "his majesty" and challenged him to apply himself, asserting that every good thing in life comes from developing and using one's mind.

Mentally I was preparing to make a point, namely, that students interested in becoming engineers should work hard in math classes; students who wished to become doctors should concentrate on chemistry and biology; and so on. I asked Charles what he wanted to be when he grew up. He smirked and replied, "I want to be a male stripper." I gave Charles an insincere smile and responded, "It's always encouraging when teachers hear students setting such lofty goals."

The teacher provided the students in blocks 1 and 2 with some very creative electronic kits, which they used to construct a variety of different working circuits. The teacher had purchased these kits with her own money, and only allowed trustworthy students to use them. Needless to say, her lesson plans stated emphatically, "DO NOT LET THE BLOCK 2 STUDENTS USE THE ELECTRONIC KITS!"

The kits contained a master circuit board, snap-together resistors, capacitors, speakers, lights, and battery units. They reminded me of the Radio Shack 150-in-One Kit that I bought my son Kerry when he was in 8th grade. I shared with the class how Kerry wired my bedroom with microphones and created a number of other nefarious devices. The block 1 and 3 eighth graders shuddered. At that age, Kerry definitely had a block 2 mentality.

At the end of the day, as I was exiting the classroom, another sub stopped me in the hall and asked, "How did block 2 go? I had them yesterday, and they were a handful! Do you know what I think should be done to those block 2 students?" He proceeded to recite a list of medieval tortures, which American schools are forbidden to use nowadays. He added another modern treatment, namely placing the subject in a cryogenic deep freeze until age 20, which sounded promising and doable.

CHAPTER 10

Pokin' a Pig

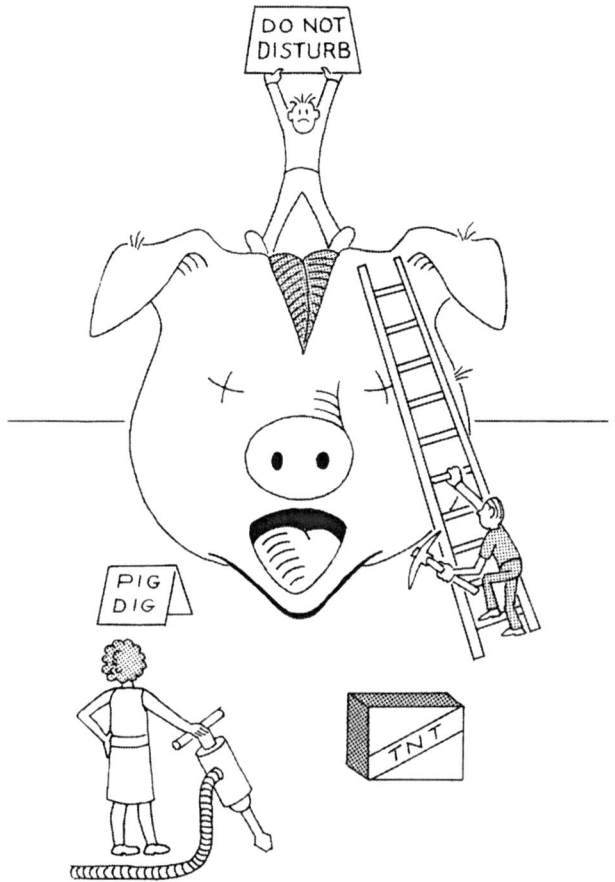

A teacher's paycheck is a room full of attentive, conscientious, and receptive students. After the block 2 experience at the mid high school, I began to wonder if the former was an impossible dream. However, in early April I drew an assignment that gave me hope. And it wasn't an April Fool's Day joke!

The high school needed a roving substitute to teach Algebra 2, the Millionaires' Club, ROTC (reserve officers' training corps), and anatomy - what a combo! As I boldly headed for the classrooms, I wondered what adventures awaited me.

Algebra 2 went smoothly. At the substitute teacher orientation class, I had designated Algebra as a preferred course. Quadratic equations and the Pythagorean Theorem are old friends to me. I helped the kids with their worksheets and answered their questions. I overheard one girl as she gave me a backhanded compliment: "Wow! They've sent us a substitute who actually knows math!"

When the bell rang, I headed for the Millionaires' Club. Never having taught this class before, my imagination ran wild. Would all the students look like Richy Rich? Would the guys wear tuxedos and top hats like the Monopoly man and the girls be dressed in diamond tiaras? Would students practice swimming in a huge vat of gold coins, like Scrooge McDuck?

When the students filed in I was relieved to see that they looked like normal kids (if one dares to declare that high school kids are normal). As they were completing their worksheets for the day, I thumbed through the textbook, and was surprised and delighted to see that the topics covered included: credit cards, insurance, the stock market, Medicare, and home financing. Apparently the name "Millionaire's Club" was meant to convey the idea that the wise use of one's resources will lead to prosperity. Who could argue with that philosophy?

Near the end of the period, I complimented the class for choosing the Millionaire's Club as an elective. I added some sage advice: "Learning works best if you apply acquired knowledge immediately after completing the class. At your age, you won't have that opportunity, so start a diary and jot down all the principles you've learned in this class. Lock it up and save it. When you start your first job (and/or get married), find your Millionaire's Club diary and let it be your financial Bible."

As I walked across the campus of Rustic Ranch High School that bright April morning, I observed quite a few young men and women dressed in Army fatigues and shiny black boots. If a campus emergency arose, would these camouflaged crusaders suddenly appear in formation and kick you-know-what? Was this the Desert Storm brigade?

When I reported for my next class assignment, I discovered where all the "Desert Storm" troopers had been heading. There they were in my classroom, seated upright in their chairs and looking alert. This was the ROTC class! Today they were conducting their yearly physical fitness tests. The test consisted of chin-ups, crunches, and a mile long jog. In order to pass the test, the cadet must complete a minimum of 4 chin-ups, 50 crunches (sit-ups), and jog for one mile. The girls substituted "holds" for chin-ups, and they had to grasp the bar and hold their body weight up for 30 seconds.

They all reassembled in a small courtyard outside the classroom for the chin-up test. One burr-topped boy did 22 chin-ups as the whole class counted - the show off! A girl held her chin to the bar for one minute, thirty seconds. After all had passed the chin-up (or chin-hold) tests, they moved indoors to a multipurpose room, dragged out mats, and finished their crunches. While they were crunching away, I noticed that this room doubled as a firing range. Uniforms and guns! No wonder the kids wanted to enroll in ROTC! After passing the crunch test, students formed ranks outdoors and jogged the one mile without even working up a sweat.

Before the bell rang they stood at attention while one very military looking lad shouted, "Ten hut!" All the boot heels clicked. "Dismissed!" And off they went to fight their battles with Biology and Algebra. The ROTC kids were so organized, I didn't have to lift a finger or blow a whistle. Our future is in good hands!

My last class of the day was the anatomy class. The regular teacher left these instructions: "Students will continue dissection of the fetal pig specimens, and when opening the skull, take care not to disturb the brain." I wondered if any previous substitutes in the anatomy class had ever vomited. Like the ROTC class, these high performers required no prodding. They went to the refrigerators, brought the zip-locked bags of pig parts to their desks, opened their little black, zippered bags (which contained scalpels and other bang-clank cutting tools), and dissected away. I felt like I was witnessing a meeting of the future surgeons of America.

The anatomy teacher left an additional instruction for me: "Collect field trip permission forms." The students were all excited about their upcoming trip to a nearby University campus. I asked one student what they planned to do at the university. She beamed and replied, "Visit the cadaver lab."

That day I crossed paths with serious students whose sights were set on careers in math, engineering, business, the armed forces, and medicine. This was a far cry from a week or so ago, when the mid high student told me he wanted to be a male stripper!

CHAPTER 11

Thoughtless

    The closing scene from my old high school movie, "The Lady or the Tiger" flashed before my eyes as I approached the room to teach ninth grade science. Would I open the door to a room full of snarling tigers (or wanna be male strippers), or would I encounter civilized, well-behaved young ladies and gentlemen? If I were in the Land of Oz, the question of the day would be "Will they be good witches or bad witches?"
    I was relieved to discover that the regular teacher was present. She taught the lesson during block 1. When the bell rang, she instructed me to teach the same lesson for the remaining blocks. (She would be gone the rest of the day, taking the block 1 students on a field trip). She apologized

Adventures of a Substitute Teacher

in advance for the block 3 kids - she said they were hard to control. Did I hear a tiger snarl, or was that just my imagination?

Block 2 went well. The kids were every bit as civilized as the block 1 students. As the students were gathering up their backpacks and waiting for the bell to ring, a sweet girl came forward to my desk and asked, "Are you going to teach the block 3 kids?" I said, "Yes." She replied, "I'll pray for you."

In the old B-Westerns of the 40's, Black Bart and his dusty gang of thugs would barge through the swinging doors of The Last Chance Saloon with guns blazing. A confrontation and brawl invariably followed, and the Durango Kid always appeared and restored law and order. As the block 3 gang swaggered into the classroom, I braced myself and silently asked myself the question, "What would the Durango Kid do in this situation?"

I tried something with the block 3 kids to break the ice. I held a brainstorming session and asked them to tell me what qualities they look for in a leader. The intent was to get them thinking positive. It is imperative in a brainstorming session that the participants have brains - or are at least willing to use what little they have. I expected "Can beat you at arm wrestling; Steals the most lunch money; Chews tobacco in class; etc." But no one had any suggestions, positive or negative.

I stared at the blank whiteboard for a moment, then turned and asked everyone in general, "Have you ever heard of the expression, 'Don't cast your pearls before the swine?'" No lights went on, although one boy asked what a swine was. The pearls of science got trampled that day! But there was a silver lining. Due to a lack of school buses, 14 of the 31 block 3 students were absent! Black Bart's gang wasn't at full force. The prayers of that sweet block 2 girl had been answered.

Later that week, I accepted a two-day assignment to teach high school science. On Thursday, there were about thirty students in each of the first three blocks. The majority of the block 4 students were scheduled to attend a Science Fair Expo, and, consequently, only seven students showed up. The assignment for the block 4 kids was, "Let them sit quietly and read." Now there's an impossible dream!

I reached into my Texas briefcase for something positive to keep the class of seven focused (and to prevent them from staging a hockey game in the back of the room). I chose the 9-magazine mind reading mystery act, which my dear old Aunt Peg had taught me 60 years ago. I picked out one of the "Magnificent Seven" and whispered the secret in his ear. The two of us spent the rest of the period baffling the other six. Before the bell rang, I shared the secret with all of them.

The next day, Friday, the fourth block was there in full force. As students filed in, I noticed a commotion in the back of the room. Suspicious that it just might be a hockey game, I raised my whistle to my lips. Just as I was about to pierce 31 sets of ears, I spied the nine-book array on the back table. The Magnificent Seven were baffling the returning Science Fair Expo classmates with the 9-magazine mind reading mystery act! I overheard another boy say that he tried it at home on his Dad and that his Dad had gotten so frustrated trying to figure out the mystery, that he cussed out his "mind-reading" son. Twenty years from now, some students might answer the question, "What did you learn in high school biology?" with "I learned a neat mind-reading trick. Wanna see it?"

Chapter 12

Safety Moment

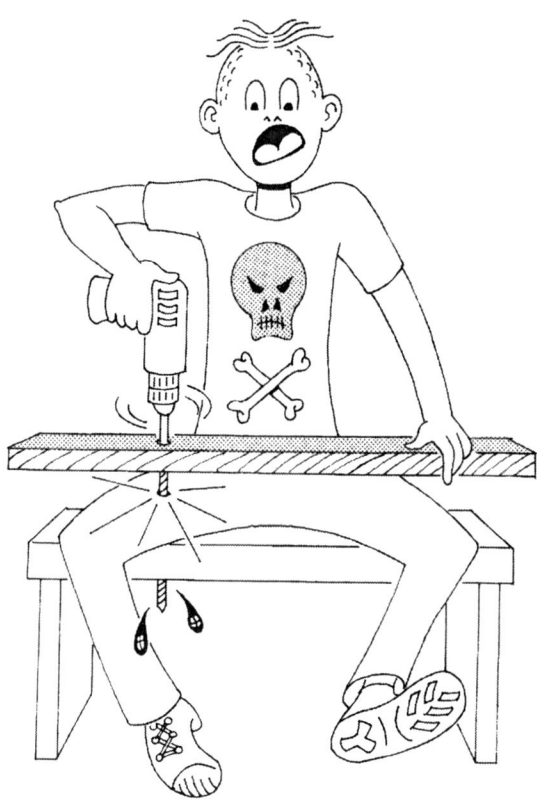

Decades ago, high schools, including the one I attended, combined grades 9 through 12 under one roof. In September, the incoming freshmen got special attention from the sophomores, juniors, and seniors, and most of it was unwelcome. Hazing was not an officially sanctioned school activity, however, it occurred, and it sent freshmen the message: "You have just become part of something bigger than yourself!" Entering high school gave ninth grade newcomers a sense of humility.

Most contemporary high schools lump grades 10 through 12 together and provide separate mid high schools for eighth and ninth graders. Ninth graders strut the halls like peacocks, unlike previous generations, who were taught to be seen and not heard and who spent their freshman year with their tails between their legs. Today's ninth graders have oversized dorsal fins and are unsinkable.

On one occasion, I accepted an assignment to teach the ninth grade Algebra class at the Rustic Ranch mid high school. I arrived early and studied the lesson plan left for me by the regular Algebra teacher. "Simple task," I thought. "Distribute Algebra worksheets; solve the problems."

When the bell rang, a flock of about 30 "peacocks" strutted through the door, presumably to study Algebra. About six sat down at a table in the back of the room. One of them pulled out a deck of cards, shuffled, and dealt. I rechecked the lesson plan. Card playing wasn't on the agenda. I got nose-to-nose with the dealer and said, "Put away the deck. If I see it again, I'll take it outside, toss it in the air, and you can play 52 pickup!" He actually looked pleased and replied, "Gee, would you?" They'll do anything to get out of class.

I distributed the worksheets and told them to get busy. The kid who remembered to bring a deck of cards to class forgot to bring his pencil. Most of his fellow students appeared to be working diligently on their Algebra assignment. I collected all worksheets just before the bell rang. I discovered that about six were blank, including the dealer's. Apparently all of the six Mississippi gamblers had forgotten their pencils, or lost them at poker game in a previous class.

Many high and mid high school teachers start their classes by assigning a problem of the day (POD). Students are required to record their answers in their journals. Teachers periodically collect the journals and grade them. The object of the POD exercise is threefold. It challenges students: to get quiet, to focus on the lesson, and to think.

My former employer at the Johnson Space Center instituted the practice of starting every meeting with a "safety moment" to impress upon employees the importance of job safety, and I suppose to get them quiet, focused, and thinking. During a safety moment, someone in the room tells the others about an experience in his or her life that caused either an injury or resulted in a "close call." A safety moment always concludes with "lessons learned," wherein the individual tells how they could have avoided the injury (or close call) by remaining alert and by paying attention to safety. Ideally the safety moment imparts wisdom to all present and puts them on guard.

I believe that safety is just as important to teens as it is to the adult workforce, and that it is never too early to promote safety. To that end, I tried starting every class with a safety moment. After taking attendance, I explained what a safety moment was and invited a student to share a personal safety moment.

A high school student volunteered. He said, "Last week I had to drill a hole in a board, so I got out the electric drill, selected the right bit, placed the board in my lap, and began drilling. The drill bit went right through the board and into my thigh. There was blood everywhere!" I asked him, "What lesson did you learn from your experience?" He replied, "Always place the board on the bench when you plan to drill a hole in it." "Perfect example," I replied.

Once the first student shared his safety moment, a dozen hands shot up. Kids were eager to share bicycle mishaps, falls, lacerations, trips, and automobile accidents. We could have stretched the safety moment into a safety marathon. I cut off the storytelling after four safety moments, and told them to get busy on the problem of the day. I only hope they didn't go home that night and stage an accident, so they could come to class on crutches or in a cast just to top their classmate's story the next time we held a safety moment.

Needless to say, the ninth graders shared some of the most bizarre safety moments. They seem to take slips, trips, and falls to a new level, but as the saying goes, "Pride (and stupidity) goeth before a fall."

CHAPTER 13

Draw Me

There is an expression, "If only he had used his talents for good instead of evil." I have been given the talent of being able to draw cartoons. In the 60's I worked at a NASA Center, and a roommate saw me drawing and asked me if I would please draw his caricature. Apparently he had been to an amusement park and had seen professional artists creating portraits for the paying customers, and perhaps he thought I'd draw his portrait for free.

To quote Webster, a caricature is "an exaggeration by means of often ludicrous distortion of parts or characteristics." My friend had a face that would warm the heart of any caricaturist worth his salt. My fingers were itching to get started. He had a high forehead, a receding hairline, an asymmetrical head shape, high cheekbones, and a nose which was narrow at the bridge and bulbous at the tip. I cautiously asked him, "Are you sure you want a caricature, rather than a portrait?" He emphatically replied, "I want you to draw a caricature of me!"

I complied. He posed while I captured him with pencil and paper. I must say that I was pleased with the resulting drawing. "Show me, show me," he said. I proudly presented him his caricature. His expectant smile melted into a disgusted frown. He alternately looked at me and the drawing, then he wadded my masterpiece into a compact ball and threw it into the wastebasket. He refused to speak to me for a week. Lessons learned: If you draw someone's caricature, never, never, never show it to them.

This experience flashed through my mind the day I subbed in a high school business computer class. A room full of kids took their places at computer terminals. The lesson plan was simple: "Ask the students to continue to work on their ledger sheets." All but two of the two dozen students were staring at the computer monitors. A native American boy was staring at his native American girlfriend with a sketchpad in one hand and a pencil in the other. He was drawing her picture. My blood ran cold!

He completed his masterpiece and showed it to her. I thought, "Prepare to learn a valuable lesson, son." She looked, she seethed, and she reacted. She wadded her caricature up in a ball, and threw it in his face. I envisioned his artist ancestor etching a petroglyph of his girlfriend, and her responding by smashing the sandstone tablet on his head. Tools and technology change, but human nature remains the same.

The kids in the business computer class, spent little time on their computers. Either they had already completed their ledger sheets and had nothing else to do, or they embraced the adage, "Never put off until tomorrow what you can put off until the day after tomorrow."

They dug into their backpacks and pulled out a smorgasbord of junk food. For the remainder of the period, they ate and snacked. When I told them I'd be with them four consecutive days, they promised to honor me by throwing a party on my last day. I said, "It looks to me like you have a party in here every day!"

I noticed that one of the boys had wheeled his chair next to a female classmate and was leaning his head against her back. I approached him and asked, "Anthony, are you listening to Jessica's food digesting? If you are, that's very perverted!" Everyone gagged and laughed. Anthony then whipped out his i-pod and earphone, pressed an earphone to Jessica's side and pretended to be using a stethoscope to improve the reception. My wisecrack elicited the desired response. The two separated.

Incidentally, day 4 came and went, without my promised party, and I recalled the line of a song from the movie, Music Man that said it all: "You can eat your fill of all the food you bring yourself." Business computer class? Maybe. Iowa picnic? Yes. Monkey business class? Definitely.

Chapter 14

Dancing with the Stars

Actor Arnold Schwarzenegger once starred in a movie called "Kindergarten Cop." In that movie, he was harassed by three dozen noisy, energetic, and uninhibited rug rats. When I accepted a two day assignment to help teach a kindergarten class, I felt like I was making the movie sequel.

This was no ordinary kindergarten class (as if any are), but a special needs kindergarten class, consisting of 8 kids with learning disabilities. All 8, however, had the unique ability to be irresistible.

The 8 so called learning disabled children had an abundance of curiosity (and nerve). I have a whistle attached to my badge lanyard. I had to fight off little fingers all day, because all the kids wanted to blow my shiny silver whistle. I also had two papers in my pocket. One contained a little map that I had drawn to help me find the school. The other had the names of the other teachers I worked with. Matthew reached into my shirt pocket and found the map. He wanted to know what it was and asked, "Can I have it?" I said, "Yes." Then Kathryn found the list of names. She not only wanted the list, but demanded that I draw another map for her on the back of the list. I was immersed in kindergarten pickpockets.

The story of the day was "Henny Penny" (the sky is falling). After reading the story, the head teacher asked me to show the kids how to draw a chicken. All eight drew their versions of a chicken pecking a grain of corn. When we drew the chicken's wing, I told the kids that they could obtain chicken wings at the local KFC. This drew a wince from the teacher, since the object of the story was to protect Henny Penny from being eaten by the fox. We added the final detail to our drawings - a falling brick, which was meant to convey the sky falling.

After completing the art project, a co-teacher put on a chef's hat and organized the next activity. She and her eight apprentice chefs were going to mix up a batch of "chicken feed." I learned the formula for chicken feed that day - peanuts, chocolate chips, sunflower seeds, raisins, and Rice Krispies.

While the kids were eating the chicken feed, the school principal's huge red Labrador visited the class. This was a fortunate turn of events, because the floor was covered with chicken feed, and the dog lapped up the spills and left the carpet spotless. A win-win situation. I didn't catch the name of the dog at the time, but in consideration of his unique talent, I think "Hoover" would be appropriate.

Hoover decided to stay for the next activity, group dancing. Eight rambunctious kids began dancing around the dog, much like savages dancing around a victim lashed to a burning pole. I feared for Hoover. How many times does this gentle creature get stepped on each day? But no! He was a conditioned veteran. He curled into a fetal position, tucked in tail and legs, and enjoyed the music. Hoover was not learning disabled.

Learning disabled children have uncanny powers of observation. During the day, I got down on the floor with them, took off my shoes, and read them stories. One child noticed the printing on the toes of my socks, "World Tour," and asked me what it meant. Another pointed to the worn spot on my heel and asked, "What's that?" These kids didn't miss a thing, which makes you wonder why they've been labeled "Learning Disabled."

Adventures of a Substitute Teacher

On my second consecutive day as "Kindergarten Cop," I realized that the honeymoon was over. On the first day, I drew a chicken for the class. On the second day, I drew recess duty, playground duty, lunch duty, and bus duty.

At recess, a little girl named Gracie recruited four of her classmates (and me) so she could play school (and be teacher). Gracie had jet black hair and a Type A (choleric) personality. I was very tempted to get a black sharpie and give her a Hitler mustache. She appointed me to be the substitute of her pretend class - I felt like I had been demoted! She ordered the substitute and her four students to sit on the cold sidewalk while she led the class. I respectfully declined. No problem. Gracie merely appointed another substitute and pressed on.

The regular teacher maintained control of the class by placing a yellow sticker on the folder of any student who acted up. It reminded me of a soccer referee showing the yellow card to player guilty of an infraction. If a child were given a yellow sticker during the week, he/she was ineligible for the Friday afternoon treat.

I was present on Friday and witnessed the treat ceremony. The teacher sat in front of the class with a "treasure chest" in her lap. Another child assisted her and distributed the treats. Gracie, whom I mentioned earlier, happened to be her assistant. The teacher had misplaced the children's folders, so she told the kids that they would be on the honor system. They would have to tell her if they had gotten a yellow sticker during the week. Immediately, Gracie piped in, "You have to tell the truth; you better not lie about it!" The teacher gave Gracie a sideways dark glance and muttered, "Gracie, it's not your job to say that."

On the wall of the room, I noticed a banner containing the three cardinal rules for kindergarten kids: 1. Be nice, 2. Do your work, and 3. Pay attention. I remarked to the teacher, "I wish I had that earlier in the week when I was teaching the high schoolers." Someone wrote a book, "All I Ever Needed to Know, I Learned in Kindergarten." Is it possible that a large percentage of the teens at Rustic Ranch high school flunked kindergarten?

At 3:45 p.m. I escorted 8 kindergarten kids to the bussing area. Since they were on four different buses, I called each of them front and center and made a chart. Putting one of these tykes on the wrong bus would ruin their day. On the chart I wrote their names, their bus assignments, and drew a little portrait of them. They loved it. Each face was the size of my little finger nail. Gracie insisted that I color the pictures, which I did. They all wanted to hold my hand on the way to the bus pick up area.

And so ended my brief career as kindergarten cop. The assignment was challenging. The pay? Chicken feed!

CHAPTER 15

Incomplete Pass

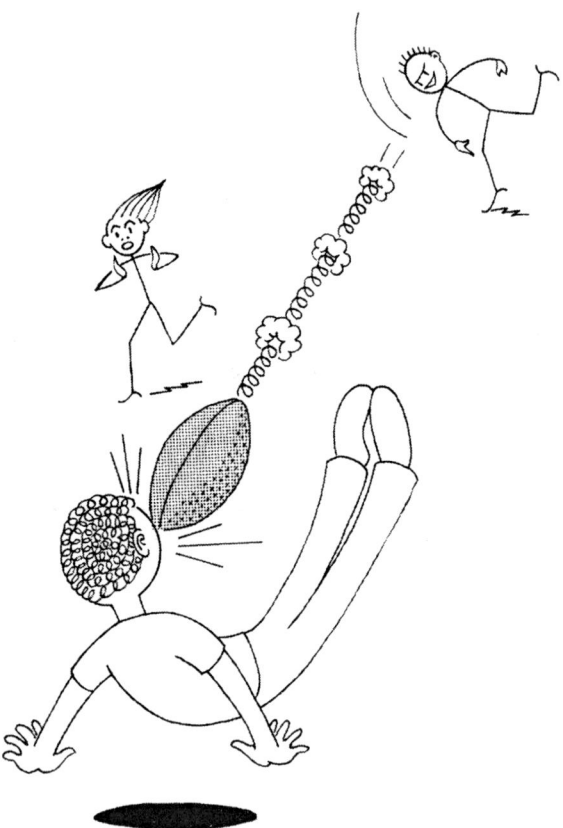

Mother Teresa operated the Sisters of Mercy ministry in Calcutta, India, where she brought light and love to the poorest of the poor. She treated each patient with dignity, as if the patient were Christ, Himself. This is Scriptural for Christ said in Matthew 25:40, "Whatever you did for one of the least of these brothers of mine, you did for me." If the patient were especially wretched or uncooperative, Mother Teresa would ask, "Lord, why have you come to me in such a distressing disguise?"

One May morning, I accepted a two-day assignment to help teach the

Adventures of a Substitute Teacher

CBI class at the Rustic Ranch middle school. CBI stands for Community-Based Instruction. There were about eight moderately to severely handicapped seventh graders in the CBI classroom. One child had Down syndrome, two were in wheel chairs, and one of these was unable to speak, move, or control her bowel movements.

As a youngster, I listened to the afternoon Adventures of Superman on the radio. When a situation arose requiring his superhuman intervention, Clark Kent spoke to himself (in an ordinary tenor voice), "This is a job for ..." then finished the sentence (in a rich baritone voice) ... "SUPERMAN!" Then it was, "Up, up, and away!" When I stepped into the classroom and surveyed the situation, I thought to myself, "This is a job for either Superman or Mother Teresa!" I met the regular teachers - they qualified as sisters of mercy.

I helped four of the kids study math and reading. Math consisted of forming numbers by connecting the dots on their worksheets. Reading consisted of connecting the dots to form letters. After forming the letters of the alphabet, we focused on the letters of their names. Then we helped them print their names. Readin' and writin' and 'rithmetic was a gargantuan task for these youngsters.

But all was not gloom and doom for the CBI kids. Although they were trapped in uncooperative bodies, they had the sparkle of life shining in their eyes, and their unbridled exuberance emerged at recess. We all went out to the playground. I attended to Nick, one of the wheelchair-bound students. Another teacher, April, brought along several other students. We two teachers supervised about six children at recess. One of the boys - George - the most articulate and physically coordinated member of the class, brought along a football.

At first George and I played catch. George threw the ball fairly well, but refrained from catching the ball, because he had a splint on his left forearm to protect a hairline fracture. I threw the ball to April, my co-teacher, who, incidentally had "good hands," and she flipped the ball to George. This is how the pro quarterbacks warm up on the sidelines - they throw and another person catches the return throws. (Oh, incidentally, April broke a nail during recess.)

Pretty soon Nick, Kelly, and Marsha wanted a piece of the action. Nick was confined to a wheelchair and had VERY limited vocabulary and communication skills. He continuously shouted, "Me, me!" which meant, "Throw me the ball, now!" I gently lobbed the ball into his lap and he wrapped his arms around it, raised it above his head with both hands, and sent it flying in unpredictable directions.

When I tossed the ball to Nick, Kelly, or Marsha, it was underhanded, without spin, and extra soft. I noticed that Marsha closed her eyes as she reached for the ball. Due to lack of coordination on the part of the CBI football team (and for safety reasons), I did all the throwing, adjusting each throw to fit the ability of the receiver.

Then something unexpected happened. Movie directors would have filmed this scene in slow motion. Marsha yelled to George, "Throw me the ball!" Up until then, I was the only person to throw to Marsha. Up until then George's tosses had been wide of the mark and "lame duck," i.e., wobbly. As fate would have it, and before I could say, "Stop!" George rifled a frozen rope, tight spiral bullet that hit Marsha smack dab in the mouth! My best receiver (April) escorted a teary-eyed Marsha to the nurse for an ice pack, and the CBI team had officially racked up its first injury - a fat lip.

When we returned to the room after recess, we discovered that we had left the door propped open. It was a windy day, and, consequently, a considerable amount of sand had blown into the classroom. There were dunes on the floor. Nick wanted to help from his wheel chair, so he grabbed the broom and started to sweep. He made many smaller dunes out of the large ones. We couldn't pry the broom away from him - we had to get brooms from other rooms for those who wanted to sweep. Two others grabbed towels and cleaned the sand off the desk tops. Every CBI kid who was physically cable of helping pitched in. They had servants' hearts and enjoyed cleaning the room. There was not a lazy bone among them.

The hope of the CBI program is to prepare students, who were never cut out to be brain surgeons, engineers, accountants, or the like, to eventually become a part of the service industry. It warmed my heart to see a servant's heart in each of these young children. I'll bet it would warm Mother Teresa's heart, too.

CHAPTER 16

Me, Me, Meat

On the second day of my CBI assignment at the middle school, I was in for a surprise. The seventh graders were taking a field trip, and the CBI children (and their teachers) were included. The destination was a Brazilian restaurant. The kids stampeded into the two school buses, and we teachers squeezed in among them and braced ourselves for a bumpy, noisy ride to the Brazilian restaurant in quintessential yellow school buses.

When riding on a bus with 50 seventh graders, you are overwhelmed by the noise. It reminded me of the crow attack in the Alfred Hitchcock movie, "The Birds." The next thing you notice is the widespread use of cell phones and text messaging devices. The students actually talk to one another on cell phones or text one another from adjacent seats. I was immersed in a chatty, audio-electronic free-for-all.

When we arrived at our destination, 200 seventh graders poured out of the bus convoy and established a beachhead in the restaurant. The scene was a cross between musical chairs and a scavenger hunt. Everyone eventually found places at the tables. I helped wheelchair-bound Nick find space at a table, and I sat beside him.

In a Brazilian restaurant, patrons select side dishes from a buffet area. Then waiters circulate from table to table, serving the meat. I went to the buffet area and loaded Nick's plate with salads, vegetables, and fruit. I delivered them to Nick, then returned to the buffet area to load my own plate.

Servers visited our table with sumptuous portions of meat on skewers. If you said that you wanted a sample, he would fork a chunk onto your plate. During the lunch period, we enjoyed at least a dozen meat selections. Whenever a server appeared, Nick shouted "Me, me, me!" This meant, "Give me a serving of that meat, pronto!" "Would anyone care for marinated beef tips?" "Me, me, me!" "Would anyone care for roasted chicken?" "Me, me, ,me!" "Would anyone care for roast beef?" "Me, me, me!" "Would anyone care for turkey wrapped in bacon?" "Me, me, me!" "Would anyone care for char-broiled pineapple?" "Me, me, me!" "Would anyone care for chicken hearts?" "Me, me, me!"

Before I realized what was happening, Nick's plate looked like a meat cornucopia. My job was to cut Nick's meat into bite sized pieces! I cut a lot of bite sized pieces that day. I instructed the servers to ignore all future "Me, me, me's" from Nick. I sure hope Nick wasn't a vegetarian.

On the bus ride back, I sat next to Kent, a 7th grade genius/prodigy. Kent and I discussed Beethoven, Egyptology, literature, Horror Films, Amusement Parks, and a lot more. I noticed that Kent was one of the few who was not using a cell phone. I asked Kent if he had a cell phone. He said, "Yes, but I have to share it with my brother." I asked, "How old is your brother?" He replied, "He's in third grade." That amazed me, so I said, "Personally, I think third graders are too young to have cell phones." He said, "So do I" and smiled at having found an ally. Silently I thought, "Seventh graders are too young to have cell phones, too."

Kent asked me, "What is your reading level?" I avoided answering the question and inquired, "What's yours?" He proudly informed me that his was somewhere between high school and college level. Kent didn't seem to have much in common with his classmates. He preferred to have an intelligent conversation with an adult. I hope I measured up to his standards.

CHAPTER 17

Pizza Mania

Falcon Crest middle school needed someone to cover for regular teachers who were taking special training. That someone was me. Middle school is composed of 6th, 7th, and 8th graders, a hodgepodge of adolescent humanity. Boys that are barely 4 feet tall with squeaky voices find themselves amidst lipstick, mascara, and panty-hose clad girls who are at least a foot taller than them.

Middle school kids enter and exit classrooms with gusto. In the movie, "Mr. Roberts," a story about the adventures of a U.S. Naval vessel crew during WWII, junior officer Jack Lemon planted a small charge of dynamite in the ship's laundry bay to annoy the ship's captain, played by Jimmy Cagney. When the charge exploded, a tidal wave of soap bubbles poured through the laundry bay door, floating everything in sight (including personnel) out the door. This best describes how middle school students entered and exited classroom doors - like a coalesced blob of humanity squeezing through a small crevasse, making it impossible for a lone human to fight the tide and go the opposite direction.

I had cafeteria duty between 11:08 and 11:38 A.M. Ninety-five percent of the kids ate pizza for lunch. The demand for pizza was so high that one of the major pizza chains had set up shop in the cafeteria. In addition, the regular cafeteria chefs made their own pizza. Friendly competition. Pizza appeared to be the "national dish" at Falcon Crest middle school. This is the age where kids are expected to have growth spurts. Vertical spurts, not horizontal.

There was an informative, two-columned poster on the wall where I was stationed. On the left, appeared the heading: HOW TO PASS. Under this heading were four bullets:

1. Show up.
2. Pay Attention.
3. Do Your Work.
4. Behave.

The heading of the right column was: HOW TO FLUNK. Under this heading were twenty-five bullets:

1. Always arrive late.
2. Always make a commotion when slipping into your seat.
3. Never have your books with you.
4. Never bring a pencil to class.
5. Never bring paper to class.
6. If you borrow paper, use it to write notes to your classmates.
7. Never ever do your homework.
8. Lose your text books.
9. Draw attention to yourself.
10. Groan a lot.
11. Say, "This is boring."
12. Ask, "Why do we have to do this stuff?"
13. After the teachers says "Turn to page 25," ask, "What page?"
14. Turn in assignments late or not at all.
15. Talk to your neighbor or stare out the window.
16. When you get an F, complain that the teacher hates you.

17. Never be concerned about your grade until the last day of the grading period.
18. If the teacher says "No," throw a fit.
19. If you are working in a group, show up unprepared, and let them down.
20. If you read in class, make it a comic book.
21. If you turn in a report, make sure to copy it word for word from an encyclopedia.
22. If you have to turn in homework, copy it from a classmate.
23. Do 5th period homework during 4th period.
24. Take no notes.
25. Stay up late; sleep in class.

Who said kids had poor memories? They can remember all 25 items from the "How to Flunk" list!

After lunch, teachers assembled the children in the corridor outside of their classrooms to discuss behavior. They told the kids that in recent weeks middle school discipline had deteriorated to dangerous levels. They explained that poor behavior would either result in: A) a behavior notice, to be sent home to their parents, or B) a write-up (which kids fear more than death). If a student gets a write-up, and is on the honor roll, he/she loses privileges accorded to honor roll students. A student (obviously not on the honor roll) raised his hand and asked, "What if you're NOT on the honor roll?" That question drew a frown and a blank look from the teacher in charge.

Another hand shot up. This was a dress code question. "We are allowed to wear red shirts. Why not pink? Isn't pink just light red?" The teacher said "Pink isn't light red and you can't wear pink."

There is a sheriff in Maricopa County Arizona that is famous for his Tent City corrections facility. Prisoners are required to live in tents, wear pink jumpsuits, pink boxers, and pink socks. Supposedly, prisoners will be sufficiently humiliated that they will never become repeat offenders. I wondered if a Falcon Crest school administrator had been a graduate of Tent City?

One more surprise about Falcon Crest middle school. Most of the teachers are women. So is the principal. The men's restroom in the teachers' lounge has a poster on the inner wall, showing five views of actress Marilyn Monroe. I guess this will remain a guy secret! Incidentally, Falcon Crest is NOT the real name of the school.

CHAPTER 18

Scarred for Life

Several decades ago, Ralph Edwards hosted the TV documentary, "This Is Your Life." Every week a guest celebrity was recognized for a lifetime of achievements. Show producers located old friends and invited these "mystery guests" to appear on the show. They would speak a few words from behind stage. e.g., "Bubba, do you remember the time we hiked up Mt. Everest together?" Then the celebrity would look wide eyed and surprised, jump up from his chair, and shout, "Could that be Mr. Keith - my high school geography teacher?" Mr. Keith usually concluded by saying, "I always knew Bubba was going to be famous and achieve great success in the world."

Some of the students I met while teaching a ninth grade Humanities class, may very well be the "Bubba's" of tomorrow. Unfortunately, they might be chained to a chair and be clad in black and white striped jumpsuits during their "This Is Your Life" moment. I got a "Bubba Alert" from the regular teacher's aide. In tones very similar to the gypsy friend of Lon Chaney (The Werewolf), she predicted, "The kids will be rowdy."

After blowing my whistle a half dozen times to quiet down the rowdies, I took attendance. Then, I introduced myself as a retired engineer from the Johnson Space Center, where the focus was on employee safety. I told them that every meeting at JSC begins with a safety moment, and I defined a safety moment. The purpose of a safety moment is to share a personal safety experience where you were either injured or came close to being injured. Then I asked for a volunteer to share his or her safety moment.

Judd was first to respond. He described his jump from a two story building that broke both legs. Lessons learned: Don't jump off roofs - gravity will get you every time.

Eddy told how he had performed daredevil tricks on his bike, and how he broke his left arm and was horrified to see the bone protruding through the skin. Lessons learned: Refrain from doing dumb things on your bike.

Carol tried to burn a plastic comb and set her hair on fire. Lessons learned: Don't play with fire.

Autumn shared how she had fallen onto the sharp edge of a railroad tie, and it had left a dent in her head. Lessons learned: Don't play tightrope walker on railroad tracks unless you are extremely well coordinated.

Ann recalled the time when an automobile ran over her leg. Lessons learned: Make sure that motor vehicle drivers see you, and stay far away from moving vehicles.

After class, Eddy rolled up his sleeve and showed us the scar from his broken arm. Autumn placed my hand on the dent in her head, and classmates lined up for a turn at feeling the dent. Ann was unwilling to show the class her crooked leg, and I was thankful for that. This was by far the most fertile safety moment discussion I'd ever had. Hands were still waving when I moved on to the next subject (Humanities).

My thoughts skittered ahead to the future and a twenty-first century equivalent of "This Is Your Life." On stage I saw a celebrity - possibly Judd, Eddy, Carol, Autumn, or Ann - being recognized for lifetime achievements. The first mystery guest was their family physician. "I never expected Judd (or Eddy or Carol or Autumn or Ann) to survive their teen years." Who knows - maybe I'll be the second mystery guest. "I never expected Judd (or Eddy or Carol or Autumn or Ann) to become a safety engineer."

CHAPTER 19

Worth a Thousand Words

When teaching at an elementary school, substitutes need guardian angels. The first thing a substitute does is to scan the teacher's lesson plan for the name of a "go-to" student, who is honest, conscientious, and helpful. The morning I reported to the Rustic Ranch elementary school to teach fourth grade, my guardian angel was a little girl named Lauren. She was at my side all day pointing out proper protocol and explaining class rules to me. I would have been lost without her.

The regular teacher had been called away unexpectedly, so the lesson plan was skimpy. I peered into my Texas brief case to search for the appropriate bang-clank equipment. I selected the cartooning lesson.

The fourth graders took to cartooning like a duck takes to water. I showed them how to draw the balloon head, how to portray facial expressions, and how to draw the stick figure. Little pencils were wiggling at warp speed.

After a child finished his or her drawing, he or she was nose-to-nose with me, proudly showing me the drawing, and hoping I would compliment them, which I always did. The kids were so enthusiastic. Several illustrated little cartoon books, stapled them together, and presented them to me.

The boys typically drew gruesome action scenes. Their stick figures held guns or knives. I think somebody needs to apply parental control to their TV sets! I wonder if the Hollywood creators of "First Blood," "Commando," and "Terminator" started out drawing stick figures in fourth grade?

As we filed to the cafeteria for lunch, several students brought along their paper and pencils, and they continued to draw cartoons on the backs of classmates ahead of them in line. I've heard of books such as "Hooked on Phonics" and now I was witnessing a "Hooked on Cartooning" phenomenon. At recess time, some pleaded to skip recess, stay in the classroom, and continue the cartooning lessons. I told the hooked on cartooning bunch, "Everyone has to go outside and get some exercise."

During recess I checked the lesson plan and discovered that we were to study botany, in particular Saguaro cactuses. I revisited the Texas briefcase for another bang-clank idea and decided that a Wheel of Fortune Game would be perfect to present information about Saguaro cactuses. I selected key phrases from the chapter on Saguaros, and those who solved the word puzzle had to answer a related question to win points. We formed three teams, played the game, answered the questions, and distributed rewards. Members of the winning team received "Smarties" candy lozenges. Members of the two losing teams received "Dum-Dum" suckers.

Near the end of the day, Carl asked, "If you were my Dad, would you teach me more about cartooning after school?" I answered, "Yes, if I were your Dad, I would." Then he asked with all sincerity, "Will you come home with me?" (That made me teary eyed - perhaps he had no Dad.) I replied, "I'm sorry Carl, but I am unable to do that." Then he said, "Will you come and be our substitute next Monday?" I replied, "Your regular teacher will be back on Monday." He wouldn't let go, and asked, "Can't you come anyway?"

The floor of the room looked like it had been ravaged by a herd of cartoonists. I urged the kids to clean the room before the bell rang.

Nobody moved. They were lined up near the door, like a column of shropshire sheep, wearing their backpacks, and giving me dumb looks. My guardian angel Lauren came to the rescue. She whispered in my ear, "You have to trick them into cleaning up the room." You need to say, "I see a piece of paper (or a book) on the floor. The first one to pick it up gets a feather." I repeated the magic words, and the kids came to life, scrambling and scavenging the floor for debris. The feather is the equivalent of a gold star. The teacher places the feathers on a poster opposite their names, and they win who-knows-what at the end of the year.

Annie drew a colored picture for me to keep and gave me a hug before leaving the classroom. Carl wanted to take me home with him. Six boys presented me with storyboards depicting bloody adventure movies, and Lauren gave me on-the-job psychology training. I left the classroom that Friday afternoon a rich man.

CHAPTER 20

Wonder Woman to the Rescue

Remember my Chapter 19 opener? ("When teaching at an elementary school, substitutes need guardian angels.") When teaching at a mid-high school, especially during the last week of school, substitutes (and regular teachers, too) need the Justice League. In case you were deprived of comic books in your youth, the Justice League consists of the entire family of DC Comic superheroes - Superman, Batman, Wonder Woman, the Flash, Green Lantern, and Hawkman.

Thursday and Friday of the last school week, I subbed for a ninth grade science teacher at the mid-high school. As the day progressed, I fully understood why she chose to skip the last two days of class.

The school day is divided into four blocks. Teachers normally hold classes during three of these blocks and use the remaining block to prepare lessons, grade papers, and catch up with administrative duties. My assignment? Teach three blocks of science. There were about 30 children in each block, so, if you do the math, I taught 90 ninth graders - ninth graders who couldn't wait for summer break. (Kids who had probably flunked this class, and who would probably be repeating it during the summer.) The kids in the first two blocks were the stuff bad dreams are made of. The kids in the last block were "worst nightmare" material.

When I surveyed the room full of "worst nightmare" ninth graders, I saw four culprits - Kenneth, Leonard, Eric, and Gene staging what appeared to be a tag team match in the back of the room. Lacking a "bat-phone," I resorted to the regular phone, dialed the principal's office, and requested back-up. Two minutes later, a uniformed security guard and an administrative official showed up and gave the four villains a stern tongue lashing. Superman, Batman, Wonder Woman, the Green Lantern, or Hawkman wouldn't have been so lenient. In my imagination, I could see four thugs tightly lashed together with Wonder Woman's golden lasso of truth, and they were red-faced, humiliated, and begging for mercy.

Bladder problems appeared to have reached epidemic proportions during the last week of school, judging by the number of kids who ask to be excused. Every time a student "needed" to leave class, I had to write a hall pass. On Thursday, I wrote hall passes: to use the restroom; to return books to library; to see the nurse; to obtain a temporary I.D.; to get something from a locker; to obtain the combination to a locker; and to pick up a hat (a boy had ordered a Philadelphia Phillies baseball cap from the media center). On Friday, I circulated through the room, pen and pad in hand, begging students to leave the room for one of the above reasons, just to reduce the noise level.

Students absorbed very little science during the last two days of school, unless signing yearbooks, blue jeans, and book bags qualify as science. The ninth grade secretary told me that one girl was having people sign her bra!

I hoped to set the tone at the beginning of class by reading Proverbs 16:32, namely, "He who is slow to anger is better than the mighty, and he who rules his spirit than he who captures a city." In other words, "Settle down and control yourselves." (It didn't work.) Matthew 7:6 tells why: "Do not give what is holy to dogs, and do not throw your pearls before swine, lest they trample them under their feet, and turn and tear you to pieces."

Near the end of the period, one of the high-spirited boys (who had apparently wriggled free from Wonder Woman's golden lasso), teased a girl beyond her human limits of endurance. She skipped the tongue lashing, bolted from her chair, and pinned the offender to the floor. I gave a silent cheer and thought, "At last, Wonder Woman has arrived and saved the day!" Should I intercede? Hmmmmm. I slowly walked toward the two and raised Wonder Woman's arm in victory.

    A moment later the brawling duo had made up and was sitting in the same chair. I went over and growled, "Unless you two are married or are Siamese twins, separate!" They complied, reluctantly. When the bell rang, Aaron was last to leave the room. He stopped, smiled at me, and said, "You controlled the class better than our regular teacher." God bless the regular teacher!

CHAPTER 21

Toilet Flush Tag

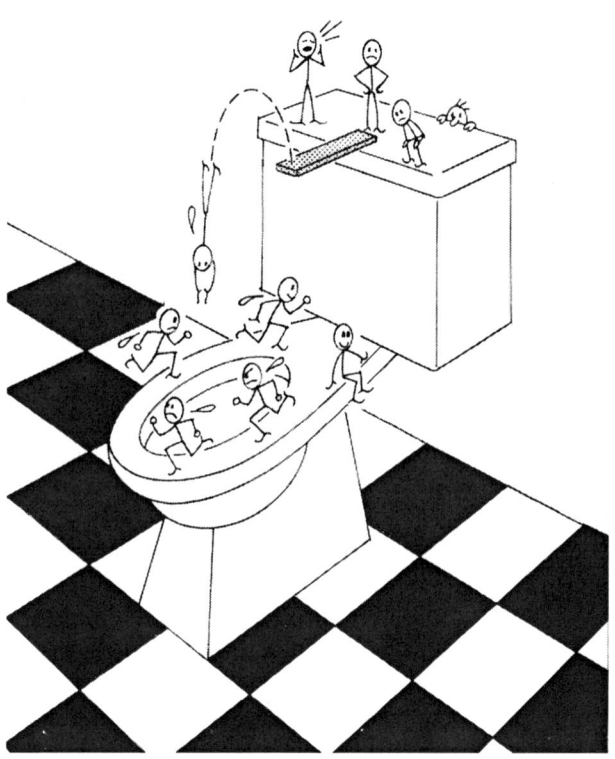

The Rustic Ranch elementary school year lasts one week longer than the high and mid-high school years, so I had the unique opportunity to witness the last day of school at both a mid high and an elementary school. I reported for duty and was assigned to co-teach an early childhood behavioral class. When I heard the word behavioral, my thoughts drifted back to the previous Friday, when I battled with 90 mid high teens, all exhibiting behavioral problems.

I was relieved to discover that there were only four children in class -

two were in kindergarten and two were in first grade. As I surveyed the class of four, I thought to myself, "Surely I won't need the Justice League today."

As it turned out, we only had the two kindergarten children for about an hour because they were pulled from class to attend a graduation ceremony. When I was in school (the typical opening line of codgers around the world), the only graduation ceremony was high school commencement. By the time my children entered school, someone had added a junior high graduation, and when my grandchildren entered school they started graduating from elementary school. Someone must own stock in a cap and gown company.

Cutting to the quick, the entire staff of the Rustic Ranch elementary school herded their students outdoors to attend the graduation of the combined kindergarten classes. Parents and grandparents were everywhere taking pictures like a bus load of Japanese tourists. About 120 little children took their seats in miniature chairs, sung patriotic songs, waved little American flags and winked to onlooking parents and grandparents, all proud as peacocks. One can only wonder if someday hospitals will hold graduation ceremonies for infants going home from the nursery.

For the rest of the day, we only had two kids in class. The situation was improving. Both first graders were tow-headed blondes. One of the other teachers said that although they were unrelated, they were often mistaken for twins. To keep them straight in my mind, I renamed them after two Rube Goldberg comic strip characters - "Ike and Mike, they look alike!"

When the lead teacher discovered my cartooning skills, he asked Ike and Mike who their favorite cartoon characters were. Ike picked Sponge Bob and Mike picked Spiderman. I drew oversized pictures of Mr. Squarepants and Mr. Arachnid on the blackboard with white chalk. Then I invited the boys to climb on stools and color their heroes with oversized rods of colored chalk. Ike and Mike held the brand spanking new chalk rods at right angles to the blackboard as they colored, and we teachers winced as they squeaked chalk in two-part disharmony. This kept Ike and Mike busy until lunch time. This "filler" activity brought to mind a childhood story that my wife Bev tells. During the long hot summers, when there was little to do, her Aunt Jeanne used to give her a bucket of water and a paintbrush. "Here, Beverly, paint the sidewalk," she'd say. By the time Beverly had painted three sections, the water had evaporated from section 1, so she'd repeat the cycle.

Ike and Mike were model students in the morning - polite, obedient, and even courteous. Too good to be true, I thought. However, they came back from lunch without their angel wings. Ike and Mike began giving one another the raspberries (a.k.a., the Bronx cheers) and were on the verge of rowdiness. In my best Professor Harold Hill imitation, I said, "Hey there! What do I hear? You both appear to have the natural ability to play a brass instrument. Make a buzzing sound like this (and I buzzed a middle C). Ike, get those cheeks in! Mike, tighten those lips!" Then I buzzed the taps, much to their delight. For the next ten minutes we worked on their embouchures, and forgot the raspberries (and the attendant spitting).

After "conservatory time," I escorted "Ike and Mike" to their Phys Ed class, where they joined other first grade students. The coach had some really creative activities for the twenty kids. After walking and jogging around the perimeter of the basketball court a half dozen times, he showed them how to play "toilet flush tag." Three kids wore colored vests and were "it." When they caught and tagged a classmate, the latter had to go down on one knee and hold up the left arm. In order for them to get back in the game, another player must sit on their other knee and push down their left arm (e.g., flush the toilet). I laughed out loud at this outrageously funny spectacle. Toilet flush tag was just vulgar enough to hold their attention.

After the Phys Ed flushing extravaganza was finished, Ike and Mike returned to the classroom, and were joined by Carlos. It was the last hour of the day, the last day of school - now what? I suggested my old standby to the lead teacher, namely a mini cartooning lesson. He encouraged me to proceed.

I taught the three boys how to draw faces and stick figures. We drew a bow-legged sheriff with a handlebar mustache, a smiling face, an angry face, and a surprised face. When the final bell of the year rang, all of them left the room clutching their cartoon creations and wearing smiley faces. Carlos asked, "Will you be back tomorrow?" I reminded him that tomorrow was Saturday. He said, "OK then, how about Monday?" "Sorry," I said, "This is the last day of school." "Oh rats!" said Carlos, losing just a bit of his smiley face.

As they say in show business, "Always leave them wanting more."

CHAPTER 22

Mouse in the House

Webster defines "special" as "distinguished by some unusual quality." The first assignment of my second season as a substitute was to teach "special education" classes at the Rustic Ranch Mid High School. Unusual? I was about to enter the Twilight Zone.

The Special Ed classes convened in portable classrooms, away from the main building. I arrived early and met the teacher's aide, who would be my co-traveler on my two day tour of the Twilight Zone. She informed me that the regular teacher was out due to the birth of his son, and that there were no lesson plans. I asked her to elaborate on the definition of special. She said that in a classroom context, special meant that the kids, for one reason or another, required special attention. They may be unable to concentrate in a large classroom, or be unstable emotionally, or lack self discipline.

The aide seemed to be in a dither. She had found mouse droppings on all of the horizontal surfaces in the room, calling for her special attention. After tidying up the place, she reported the problem to the custodians, hoping they would rid the portable of the pesky rodent! As it turned out, the special problem would be solved in an unusual way by a special person.

During the second period, Jack, one of the 8th grade students, was in the back of the room returning a book to the shelf. He happened to look over a room divider and spotted a furry little mouse taking a nap in the coils of the refrigerator. Jack, who claimed to be a skillful handler of furry creatures (he had previously told the class about his pet tarantula spider) crept around the divider and grabbed Mr. Mouse. At that very moment the fire alarm sounded! Things like that happen in the Twilight Zone.

There were eight of us in the portable, and we all filed out and headed for the assembly area, a long sidewalk adjacent to the mid high baseball field. Jack was clutching a frightened mouse. Our eight special kids joined hundreds of other kids, who were lined up along the sidewalk. Jack placed the mouse on the ground, and it immediately scampered down the sidewalk, skittering across the tops of everyone's shoes. You could tell the location of the mouse by checking to see which kid was air-born.

Some of the more bloodthirsty students shouted "Stomp on it!" One tender-hearted teacher ran alongside the mouse, like a football coach following a player down the sidelines. She pleaded, "Don't hurt it! Don't hurt it!" As far as I know, the mouse survived and, if mice think, thought he had a very unusual - even special - day.

We returned to the portable and the subject "What do you want to do when you get out of school?" came up. I remembered a similar discussion from the previous school year in a classroom at this very same school. A boy told me he wanted to be a male stripper. One of today's Twilight Zone boys topped this. He said he was looking for a job where he could blow things up. I tried to steer him away from a career in terrorism and advised him to join the army and get into demolition. Be all you can be.

Most of the half dozen denizens of the Twilight Zone had next to zero attention span. I had an idea. Play a game and give them treats. The game I had in mind was "Wheel of Fortune." I explained the rules to the class and apologized because we lacked a wheel, lacked a fortune, and lacked Vanna White. But when visiting the Twilight Zone you have to improvise!

I drew a pattern of blank lines on the whiteboard representing phrases taken from their U.S. History text. The kids guessed a letter. If it were present, I printed it in the appropriate space, if not, another kid guessed a letter. The kids grumbled, "Hey! This isn't Wheel of Fortune. It's hangman!" I reminded them, "Whatever you want to call it, always remember, there will be treats" (the magic words). They paid attention and played the game.

At the end of the game, Brent, who was a six foot five, 300+ pound member of the mid high football team created a puzzle for the class. He was hoping to baffle me. He carefully drew a pattern of lines on the board. Jack guessed the first letter, "R." There were two R's. Jack guessed an "I." There were three I's. Jack's next guess was unsuccessful. Brent turned to me and said, "OK, teacher, you guess a letter." I said, "May I please solve the puzzle?" He frowned. I guessed: "RUSTIC RANCH MID HIGH IS THE BEST." Brent was really disgusted and grumbled something derogatory about teachers. Bad psychology on my part. I should have made him feel good by playing dumb and eking out the letters one at a time.

The kids were special, the events were unusual, and the outcome was positive. A rare treat for a substitute teacher traveling through (mystery music, please) the Twilight Zone.

CHAPTER 23

Ambience

Every classroom has an ambience. Webster (him again?) defines "ambience" as "a feeling or mood associated with a particular place, person, or thing: ATMOSPHERE."

Teachers go to great lengths to fashion a classroom environment that will facilitate, foster, and further the educational process. A teacher will spend all summer playing architect, interior designer, art collector, and psychologist, so that in the fall, every square inch of the classroom will be aglow with ambience.

On that first day of school the observant student will see the

American flag; an oversized calendar; colorful posters; portraits of the Presidents; scientific charts (including the Periodic Table of the Elements); positive thinking slogans; decorator lamps; curtains at the windows; cozy book corners with plush pillows and bean bag chairs; and plastic tubs and baskets of every size brimming with art supplies, calculators, and pencils. Did I say the observant student? All too frequently, i-pod obsessed children file into the room with their thumbs locked at a ninety degree angle and their heads locked in the "down" position, and the carefully crafted ambience literally goes right over their heads. I'll bet some students wander through the whole year without reading a single poster.

My wife and I taught Vacation Bible School during the summer. The theme was "Preaching the gospel in a tropical rain forest." Ten teachers turned ten classrooms into tropical rain forests. There were elaborately painted backdrops showing mountains, volcanos, flora, and fauna; floor-to-ceiling cellophane waterfalls; cardboard monkeys and fat snakes hanging from the ceiling; giant spiders and lizards pasted to the walls; rows of bamboo shoots sprouting from the floor; tents and camping equipment in the corners; and smiley teachers in the doorway wearing pith helmets. The VBS staff had achieved the apex of ambience. (I-pods were checked at the door.)

On my second assignment of the new school year, I taught 6th grade math at a middle school. When I walked into the room, the ambience was overwhelming! I spotted: 1) an Ohio State University (OSU) throw rug in the front of the room, 2) an OSU pennant on the wall, 3) an OSU megaphone on the desk, and 4) lip balm with an OSU logo on the file cabinet. I was subbing for a brother (actually sister) Buckeye!

The sixth graders could never have responded to the scarlet and gray memorabilia like I did. Visions of the past flashed through my mind: Columbus, Ohio; the Olentangy River; High Street; Mirror Lake; the horseshoe-shaped Buckeye football stadium; the oval campus with its crisscrossing sidewalks; Orton Hall and the campus chimes; University Hall, the Thompson Library; the Ohio State University Marching Band performing their famous ramp entrance and executing the Script Ohio formation; the senior sousaphone player dotting the "i" ... and to think, all this from a throw rug! Ambiance is a powerful force.

Although I had never met the teacher, I felt a kinship with her and was determined to say thanks for the ambience. I plotted a conspiracy with the students in her classes. I taught them the OSU song, "Round on the Ends and High in the Middle." The next day when their teacher returned, one of the musically-gifted students, Jan, was to step to the front of the room and conduct the "6th grade Buckeye choir" as they sung this special song to their teacher. I'd like to think that they remembered to do this, and that the teacher was surprised, elated, and got teary eyed with sentiment. I'd like to think that, but we were dealing with 6th graders and the adage "in one ear and out the other" kept haunting me.

Later that day I monitored a study hall full of 6th graders. The schools call these free-for-alls "advisory periods." (My advice to the school would be to eliminate advisory periods.) The rules are simple during advisory periods. Kids have to keep quiet (ha, ha), complete assignments and worksheets from their other classes, and/or read books.

In an effort to promote book-learning and kindle interest in reading, I shared the story of my 6th grade literary club and the contest to see who could read the most books during the school year. Back in the late 40's kids responded to contests, competed to sell seeds for the PTA, held money-making raffles for "swell prizes," and worked hard to read the most books. My two sixth grade teachers promised our class a surprise treat if everyone read his or her quota of books.

When the year was over, the teachers tallied up the points to determine who had read the most books. Teachers had compiled a list of approved books, so we couldn't merely read a Dick and Jane book to earn credits. The harder (and more boring) the book, the higher the point value. You can be sure that "War and Peace," "A Tale of Two Cities," "Oliver Twist," and "The Three Musketeers" were at the top of their list.

The surprise treat was a class party. That was the good news. The bad news was, boys had to ask girls to attend. The worst news was, there would be dancing, and everyone had to change partners during the party. The advisory period boys gagged and gasped. So did the girls. I told them that boys and girls responded the same way in my 6th grade class. Ha!

We talked about the rewards of reading for its own sake, and I called their attention to the whiteboard where I had written: "Man's mind, once expanded by a new idea, never returns to its original dimensions." I challenged them to continue their reading and studying, for no one could take away their educations. I glanced around the room to see what kids were reading. A lot of Dick and Jane category books! I imagined that I saw scores of heads actually shrinking!

CHAPTER 24

Excuses, Excuses

In the movie "Only the Lonely," John Candy wanted to take a very bashful Ally Sheedy out on a date. Ally was so bashful, she was speechless. John Candy, ever gentle and resourceful, said, "I'll make this easy for you. I'll give you a list of excuses why you can't go out on a date with me this Saturday. All you have to do is nod your head for yes or shake it for no." He began, "You're seeing someone else?" Ally shook no. "You're having your wisdom teeth removed?" (No.) "You're washing your hair?" (No.) "You're going shopping?" (No.) "You have to baby sit your niece's kids?" (No.) "You're doing your laundry?" (No.) "You're lubricating your car?" (No.) "You're waxing your legs?" (No.) John concluded, "Then you really will be able to go out with me on Saturday?" She smiled and nodded yes.

The last Thursday and Friday of August I was called to teach math to 5th graders at the Rustic Ranch elementary school. I discovered the excuses why 5th graders can't do their math worksheets.

Excuse 1: We have to check out your Texas briefcase.

A curious little girl named Amy spotted my Texas brief case, which was loaded with my bang-clank teaching aids, and she was fascinated by it. She asked, "What's this?" I replied, "My teaching supplies." She continued, "Can I see what's inside?" I said, "Not now." She went on, "May I lift it to see how heavy it is?" "Anything to get her back to her seat," I thought. "OK." Before I knew it, all 30 kids were in line waiting to hoist my Texas briefcase off the floor.

Excuse 2: Zach's tooth is loose.

As I scanned the room, the math worksheets remained untouched. The attention had shifted from my Texas briefcase to a boy named Zach, who had his hand in his mouth. Loose tooth! Out it popped to the ooh's and ah's of the entire class. I provided Zach with some cotton balls and a zip lock bag, and he put the tooth and the cotton balls in the bag and headed for the school nurse. Meanwhile two little girls at his table sterilized their hands with liquid hand cleaner. Moments later Zach returned with a miniature, orange-colored, plastic treasure chest that the school nurse had given him. In it was his bloody tooth, ready to be transported home and placed under a pillow. More drama than a Broadway play, but still the math worksheets remained untouched.

Excuse 3: I have to protect myself from Andy.

Only one child in math class should have been caged. His name was Andy. I noticed that he was constantly bothering a boy named Ron. Neither boy had written so much as a plus or minus sign on his worksheet. Hurricane Gustov and Hurricane Hannah were disrupting the Atlantic and Gulf Coast that week. Double trouble. Andy and Ron were disrupting the classroom. I confined Andy and Ron to their chairs and set them to work on their math worksheets. To my great surprise and delight, Ron completed both worksheets in nothing flat!

Excuse 4: I am an evil genius.

As far as I could tell, Ron was the only one to finish his math worksheet. That was the good news. The bad news was, now he was alongside me at my desk striking up a conversation. He opened by asking me trick questions (to see how dumb I was). Next he tried to impress me with his vast knowledge of birds of prey. Ron informed me that he wanted to become a zoologist and study animal life on the continent of Australia! At first I thought, "That beats being a male stripper or a person that blows things up!"

I changed my mind when Ron told me about his recent trip to the zoo. He said, "I stood nose to nose with a baboon." (The baboon was behind a glass wall.) From the story, I got the impression that Ron had stared down and taunted the poor creature to the point that the baboon would have given a month's ration of bananas if he could have broken the glass and throttled Ron. Mercifully, Ron's Mom dragged him away. I was tempted to let Andy get back out of his chair and sic him on Ron.

Excuse 5: (perhaps the only legitimate reason) I have no interest whatever in math.

A gaggle of giggly girls pretended like the math worksheets on their desks were invisible. They chatted, smiled, giggled, and wasted the whole class period. Given the opportunity and the wax, their excuse for not doing their math worksheets could have really been: "We're waxing our legs!"

CHAPTER 25

The Purple Circle

As a kid I loved to peruse the Johnson Smith Company's catalog. For a fraction of a dollar you could own: an X-Ray machine, a live alligator, a book on ventriloquism, a book on wooing the ladies, a bike-o-motor, a levitating mummy, magnetic dogs, and thousands of other intriguing toys. I sent for the magnetic dogs. The set included two plastic 3/4 inch long dogs, one white and one black, glued to bar magnets. When you placed them nose-to-nose on a flat surface they separated, spun around and snapped together in the nose-to-tail configuration.

Every time I have taught at the high or mid high schools, I am reminded of my old magnetic dogs toy - the students are holding hands, hugging, kissing (thankfully nose-to-nose), and walking arm-in-arm between classes. In class there is a lot of sitting on laps and clustering. I often wondered why school districts didn't offer classes on inappropriate touching in public (not how to do it, but why they should avoid it).

As it turns out, the district does offer such a class, and I witnessed it during the first week of September, when I subbed in the Special Needs class at the middle school. The social studies teacher visited the classroom to talk about personal space. She brought her own bang-clank equipment, consisting of a video tape and a large piece of oilcloth imprinted with a seven-foot diameter pattern of multicolored concentric rings.

At the center of the pattern was a purple circle 18 inches in diameter. The social studies teacher stood one of the seventh graders in the inner circle and said, "Children, the purple circle represents your personal space. No one may come into your personal space without permission - NO ONE!" Then she asked the class, "Who may come into your purple space without permission?" The class chorused their reply, "No one!" "Good answer, good answer," said the teacher.

She then showed a video that further illustrated the importance of respecting the other person's personal space and of demanding respect for your own personal space. Around the purple circle were concentric circles of green, red, blue, etc. Each, I presumed, represented degrees of trust, and each had its own set of guidelines, and these areas would be covered in sequence on future visits.

I wondered if this lesson made any long term impact on the students. Based on what I've seen in high and mid high schools, I'd say that quite a few need a remedial course on purple circles. Did it make a short term impact? I got the answer that same day while I escorted the kids to PE and lunch. The kids broke ranks and began pushing and punching their classmates. I played conscience and kept reminding them to stay out of one another's purple circles. The prime offender was Matt, who would likely never learn the lesson of the purple circle. I could just picture him as the new seventh-grade super villain - "The Purple Marauder."

This was a two-day assignment for me. On the afternoon of the first day, the special needs class took a field trip. Ten kids and five teachers walked single file from the school to the local grocery store, which was about 0.8 miles from the school. The purpose was to buy ingredients for a "fruit pizza," to be made the next day.

When we arrived at the store, we formed teacher-student teams. Each team had to find the items on their shopping lists. I ended up with three boys, and the items we needed were strawberries, M&M's, eggs, and wax paper. My job was to keep up with three hyperactive seventh grade boys, who were shoving a shopping cart at warp speed. This was probably a rerun of an experience Mrs. Howard (mother of the The Three Stooges) must have had when she took Moe, Shemp, and Curly shopping!

The kids were also allowed to buy something for themselves with their own money. One kid named Gabe had ten dollars with him. The other two kids on the team helped him spend his money (and also cajoled him to buy them some goodies as well). At the cash register, I overheard another teacher exclaim rather enviously, "I don't even have ten dollars myself, and I'm the adult here!"

On the walk back to school, I told a boy named Mark that I collected rocks. He immediately noticed gravel in the driveways and tree lawns. Mark asked permission to pick up a small piece of white gravel from a tree lawn. I presumed that this would be the first rock in his collection.

The second day was fruit pizza day. The teacher taped the recipe (and all the steps) to the white board; directed the kids to get out all the supplies (flour, sugar, baking soda, milk, margarine, bowl, cups, teaspoon, paddles, forks, etc.); and walked them through the process of making sugar cookies. The cookie would be the crust for the fruit pizza. The children took turns adding and stirring the ingredients. The biggest challenge for the teachers was preventing the kids from sneezing into the mixing bowl. One happy little guy sang throughout the whole event, and we tried to keep him from singing directly into the bowl.

Once the dough was finished the teacher scooped out softball-sized dollops onto squares of wax paper. She had written the kids' names on the waxed paper. We placed these on cookie sheets, and put them in the ovens (we were across the hall from the food lab, so we were able to use about 5 ovens). While the (female) teachers were merrily loading the cookie sheets into the oven, I put on my resident safety engineer hat and asked, "Won't the waxed paper catch fire in the oven?" My inquiry just received dumb looks.

After the cookies had been in the oven for about ten minutes, rivulets of smoke started curling up from each oven! Panic! We donned the oven mittens, slid the cookie sheets from the ovens, flipped over the charred dough, and removed the waxed paper. That's when all traces of ownership vanished.

Luckily there were no fires, and no smoke detectors were triggered. We baked on for another 20 minutes. The results were a dozen 10-inch diameter, inch-thick, pancake-shaped sugar cookies. Some were scorched on one side (we concealed the evidence by turning scorched sides downward when we put them on the paper plates).

The kids decorated their cookies with strawberries, bananas, canned icing, grapes, maraschino cherries, and M&M's. Some actually ate the whole cookie! I took a small wedge (maybe a sixth of a cookie), decorated it to look like Mr. Bill's head, and enjoyed my Friday afternoon treat with the others. The lead teacher, at my suggestion, borrowed a camera and photographed each child with his or her creation. Even the "Purple Marauder" baked a cookie, but predictably, he entered the cookie's purple space as he was icing it and got icing all over his nose.

CHAPTER 26

Tour of the Universe

According to President Franklin Delano Roosevelt, "December 7, 1941" (the day the naval and air forces of the Empire of Japan suddenly and deliberately attacked the United States of America) was "a date which will live in infamy." December 7, 1941 wasn't the only date to live in infamy. September 8, 2008 also vies for that title. It was the day I taught 9th grade science at the Rustic Ranch mid-high school.

At the substitute teacher orientation, I indicated that science was one of the subjects I preferred to teach. On the way to school, I was elated to have finally been given the opportunity to teach science. The science class was focusing on astronomy, in particular the galaxies, and deeply nestled in my Texas briefcase was my coveted Power Point presentation of the Hubble Telescope's deep space photographs.

The school secretary generously provided me with a computer, a digital projector, and a screen. I inserted the disk and began the Technicolor tour of the known universe. My expectations were astronomical. The ninth grade response was microscopic. After the cosmic dust settled, the biblical expression about pearls before pigs reared its ugly head again - third time this year.

Politicians on the campaign trail always seem to be concerned about solving America's education problems. They maintain that the solution to the education problem is "better teachers and more money to the schools." It is true - the United States does have an education problem. Based on the results of a 2002 UNICEF survey, the United States ranked 18th among nations in the "percentage of 15 year-olds falling below international benchmarks." The top six nations in this survey were: South Korea, Japan, Finland, Canada, Australia, and Austria.

Wouldn't it be a political eye-opener if politicians were required to serve a week (or month) teaching school before offering any bold solutions to the education problem? I'd put them with ninth graders. They would soon discover that kids who place no value on education, who are too rude to be teachable, or who are too lazy to take advantage of a learning opportunity will not smarten up no matter how much money is pumped into their school or how many advanced degrees their teachers have earned.

After weathering 7 periods of chatter and disinterest in the world-class Hubble tour of the universe, I realized that part of the problem may simply be mechanical - the way students were seated in the classroom. Tables were oriented such that twenty-five percent of the kids had their backs to the teacher, and had to turn their heads 180 degrees to make eye contact (OK for owls - a little tough for humans). Fifty percent were seated with their ears pointing to the front of the room; they had to turn their heads ninety degrees to make eye contact with the teacher. Only twenty-five percent of the class was actually facing front.

When the eighth period students entered the room, I informed them that we were going to perform an experiment. I rearranged the tables into two long rows and directed the students to sit on one side of the table, all facing me. That seemed to make a big improvement. I had eye contact with everyone. The only hitch was, when the lights went out and I began the slide show, I saw a white shirt under one of the tables. Apparently one of the boys felt that he needed to take a nap during 8th period. I announced to the class that this was the first student that had ever expired in one of my classes and that we'd better call the mortician. The culprit was embarrassed, got up, sat in his seat, and "caught the tour bus" as the Andromeda Galaxy appeared on the screen.

Most of the day lived in infamy, but by changing the seating in eighth period, we had managed to accomplish "one small step for man."

CHAPTER 27

Gumming Up the Works

The first Friday in September, I taught at the high school. As I was walking from the parking lot to the administration building, I noticed that the sidewalks appeared to be speckled. Upon closer examination, the specks were actually thousands of chewing gum fossils. That made me think of the first scientific paper I ever wrote. As a member of the Space Sciences Division at the Jet Propulsion Lab, I studied the crater frequencies on the moon in an attempt to date prominent features. The results were published in the Journal of the Astronomical Society of the

Pacific under the title, "Dating Lunar Surface Features by Using Crater Frequencies."

In my study, I assumed that the influx of meteorites over the lifetime of the earth and moon was constant and isotropic. The collision frequency was based on recovered meteorite falls in heavily populated areas. Using that approach, I was able to determine the ages of large surface features such as the continental area and Mare Imbrium.

This got me thinking. Could we set up a hidden camera on campus, measure the amount of gum discarded by "X" students within a set time, assume that students in the past had consumed and discarded gum at the same rate, count the gum fossils in a test area ("Y") and come up with an age for that particular section of sidewalk?

Maybe I could get federal funding to do the study. Or I could just ask school administrators when the school was built and subtract that date from the current date!

My assignment that Friday was to teach several subjects, including: Advisory Period (study hall), Creative Writing, Yearbook Staff, and Newspaper Staff. This sounded like the perfect assignment! But I have learned to be very suspicious of perfect assignments. The last one - teaching ninth grade astronomy - almost spiraled me into a black hole of student apathy.

The Advisory Period went as expected. Three categories of kids showed up:

Category 1 kids actually studied - they used their time for good.
Category 2 kids harassed one another and did clandestine things - they used their time for evil.
Category 3 kids went into suspended animation - time was nonexistent.

Students in Advisory are allowed to leave the room and go to another location to receive tutoring for subjects they have fallen behind in. When I substitute in an Advisory period, I try to seek out the Category 2 kids and encourage them to leave class and find a tutor. There have been some Advisory periods when I just asked them to leave class, period! The ideal Advisory period would be one where every kid was a Cat 1. But when push comes to shove, I'll settle for a room full of Cat 3's - zzzzzzz!

When I showed up to teach Creative Writing, there were no lesson plans. Some of the students said they knew what they were supposed to do. When a fox sneaks into the hen house, he too knows what he is supposed to do. I suspected that they didn't know what to do, so I decided to give them a concrete assignment.

It takes great creativity to write a resume - ask any person who is out of work. These kids were taking creative writing. I expected them to be creative and to enjoy writing. I challenged them to pick a historical personality and to write his or her resume in such a way that the person would qualify for a modern job. I told them that we had a time machine, and that we would be retrieving them from the past and be bringing them forward to the year 2008. On the whiteboard, I wrote a list of six famous men and six famous ladies. They were allowed to use computers to check out their clients' backgrounds and achievements.

One of the men on the list was Attila the Hun. I was hoping one of the boys would be creative and write a catchy resume for Attila, and consider submitting it to the Chicago Bears in response to a want-ad for a linebacker. The response to my creative writing challenge was a chorus of yawns. If I had a cold mirror, I would have checked their respirations. Hey! I looked closely at their faces. They looked a lot like the Category 3 kids from the Advisory period - zzzzzzz!

During Newspaper period, I asked the editor if they had a cartoonist. He rounded up one eager-eyed lad, and I gave him a quick tutorial on how to draw cartoons. We talked about drawing caricatures, and I told him about my unpleasant experience of drawing my best friend's caricature, which caused a breach in our friendship. I said, "My friend had begged me to draw his caricature, and, when he saw it, he tore it up and refused to speak to me for a week." The Newspaper student, undaunted by my warning, said, "Will you draw MY caricature?" What the heck! Things were slow. I drew it, but made it simple and flattering. He thanked me with a broad smile - just like the one I put on his caricature!

The other kids in the Newspaper class knew what they should have been doing, but instead, chose to apply makeup, tease one another, and avoid eye contact with the substitute teacher. One girl sat talking to her friend the whole period. Every other word was an obscenity. My report to the teacher contained a compliment: "Julie was the most accomplished and fluent cusser I have ever heard." I wondered what column she wrote for the newspaper - the cussified ads?

In the movie, "The Music Man," Professor Harold Hill taught Marion's little brother Winfred how to whittle and spit. On Friday afternoon, I left the Rustic Ranch high school confident that someone had taught the students how to chew gum and cuss. (And it wasn't me.)

CHAPTER 28

Where Angels Fear to Tread

During the third week of September I agreed to help teach the CBI class at Rustic Ranch High School. CBI stands for community based instruction. I had previously taught a CBI class at the middle school. On Monday I reported to Mrs. Huss for duty. She asked me if they told me about this class when I accepted the assignment. I said (with some apprehension), "No." Then Mrs. Huss gave me the following warning: "Reggie was in a mental institution - if he panics, it will take ten men to subdue him; Theodore vomits daily - so always have a waste basket handy to catch the fluids; Kathy pulls hair - luckily, mine was too short for her to grab; and Wendell bites, kicks, head-butts, and hits - don't ever let him get behind you!"

Theodore, who had cerebral palsy and was unable to speak, arrived in his wheel chair at about 9:00 A.M. At 9:02, he vomited - yards away from a waste basket! He sat on the floor with legs spread apart to avoid soaking his pant legs in the 18 inch pool. The teacher gave the custodian a 911 call. Another Einstein time dilation occurred - minutes seemed like hours. Meanwhile the other students and teachers were groaning and gagging at the smell. (Since I've lost my sense of smell, it wasn't that bad for me.) Finally the custodian arrived with bucket and mop. I thought, "What's next? The day has just begun!"

Wendell was autistic and was either unable to speak or chose to remain silent. He did, however, walk. Mrs. Huss said that if she were to walk as much as Wendell, she'd have blistered feet.

My sons like to compete against one another in computer racetrack simulations. They have steering wheels that hook into their computers. They select a famous racetrack, e.g., the Indianapolis 500, then "drive" around that track at breakneck speeds. Wendell had a track he followed around the room. If you looked closely at the carpet, you could almost see it. There were a few "out of bounds" areas. The teacher placed purple tape on the floor to stake out her desk and work area. Wendell knew that this was off limits to him, but when Mrs. Huss wasn't looking (which was rare) he'd put one foot over the line to rattle the staff.

Kathy, who had Down syndrome (DS) and was also unable to speak, spent most of her day napping on what appeared to be a giant bean bag, located in the center of Wendell's walking track. (The bean bag was also off limits for Wendell.) Kathy got up and joined the class for group learning activities and lunch - she got up especially fast for lunch! Kathy made mono-syllable sounds throughout the day - her favorite being "eeoow."

At 10:00 A.M. six more Down syndrome children joined the class for a science lesson. The teacher pulled the table away from the wall and arranged the chairs to accommodate the larger group. The table and chairs blocked the track, and this irritated Wendell. He suddenly and deliberately slapped one of the visiting Down syndrome students (Allan) on the back of the neck, causing him to cry. I took Allen to the school nurse for an ice pack. He lay on a cot, and I stayed with him to help calm him down. Meanwhile the teacher called security, who escorted Wendell outside for a few laps around the campus. When Miss Martin, the regular teaching aide saw me looking wide-eyed and amazed, she smiled sadistically, and said, "Welcome to our world."

On Tuesday, I reported back for another day - much to the surprise and delight of the head teacher and the other three aides. I think they expected me to go AWOL. Theodore had the dry heaves shortly after he arrived (we had a waste basket in his lap in three nano seconds). Wendell decided not to hit anyone on Tuesday, but he did walk another thousand miles, grinning and flashing 28 sharp teeth, reminding me of the alien from the movie of the same name.

The social study topic that day was getting along with others. I had, in my Texas briefcase, a concentration game called "Ten Tips for Making Friends." When the six DS kids joined us, Mrs. Huss invited me to play the Ten Tips game with the class. They were exhilarated, elated, and exuberant! Every time a student guessed two cards that matched, they whooped, hollered, and clapped so loudly that security guards burst into the room, fearing a riot. When they saw everyone seated around the table, eyes riveted to the pegboard and cards, they grinned, shook their heads and left.

Tuesday was recipe day. Miss Martin (an aide) brought in her recipe for creamy apple crisp. The DS kids joined us and everyone (except Wendell who was continuing his marathon around the room) sat around the table, taking turns cutting the apples, adding the ingredients, and stirring the mixture. I quietly kept my eye on Theodore, the thrower upper. Earlier that morning, he had sneezed so violently that gobs of snot went every which way. It reminded me of the scene from Jurassic Park, where the brontosaurus got eye to eye with the two kids sitting on the limb, then sneezed all over them. When it came Theodore's turn to stir the mixture, Mrs. Huss said, "Theodore has long arms - keep the bowl at arm's length and away from his nose."

After the creamy apple crisp had baked for twenty minutes in the toaster oven, we all sat at the table and sampled it. I warily took a very small portion, wondering if any extra ingredients had been added!

Wednesday went fairly well - no vomiting, no hitting, no security busts! We played the concentration game again with much the same results. We also played monopoly, which turned out to be a hands on lesson in entrepreneurship for Reggie, who operated an oversized calculator and served as the banker.

Thursday was so action-packed, I don't know where to begin. Shortly after Theodore arrived, he vomited, and even though we had him straddling a wastebasket, he managed to miss. Wendell tried to kick Miss Martin and took another tour of the campus with the security guards. Not to be out-shined by Theodore and Wendell, Kathy, whose only offenses had been noisemaking and burping, decided to pee on the bean bag chair! Clorox wipes were moving at warp speed. Kathy's parents had failed to include a change of clothes in her back pack. Miss Martin went on a scavenger hunt and found a pair of sky-blue satin bloomers in another classroom. Kathy, flamboyantly wore the blue satin bloomers for the duration.

At about 2:00 P.M., two school busses arrived, and between 30 and 40 CBI students and their teachers climbed aboard to go bowling. The busses were equipped with lifts so four kids in wheel chairs came along, too. At the bowling alley, Theodore joined the three other kids in wheel chairs and "bowled." Lane personnel installed gutter-guards in lane 1, and they placed a special stainless steel chute at the scratch line. The kids wheeled themselves up to the chutes, a teacher placed the bowling ball at the top of the chute, the kids pushed the ball down the chute, and the ball rolled down the lane and knocked over the pins.

Theodore had been hyped up about the field trip all morning, but when we positioned him at the chute, he seemed more interested in ogling the Sponge Bob poster on the wall next to lane 1, than knocking down the pins. In spite of the distractions, Theodore scored 106, which is better than I usually do when I go bowling.

One little DS girl in an adjacent lane launched her tangerine-colored ball with a weak push. It took an eternity to reach the pins. One time it stopped midway down the lane. An attendant fetched it back and gave her a do-over.

On the way to the Bowling Alley, I sat behind a boy named Aaron. When he spotted my Ohio State badge lanyard, he lit up and told me that he was a Buckeye fan. He asked, "May I sit with you on the return trip back to school?" I said, "OK." Aaron happened to be reading a book about The Ohio State University, and he asked me a hundred questions about the OSU Campus, Woody Hayes, the Ohio State football team, the Marching Band, and the traditions. I told him as much as I could remember (which was considerable).

The rivalry between Ohio State and Michigan is legendary. As part of this tradition, Buckeyes have a song they sing at the OSU-Michigan football game. I taught this song to Aaron: "Oh, we don't give a damn for the whole state of Michigan, the whole state of Michigan, the whole state of Michigan, we don't give a damn for the whole state of Michigan, we're from OHIO." He memorized it. As he got off the bus, he shouted, "O - H" and I echoed, "I - O!" Outside the bus, Aaron told his teacher, "Next time you take a day off, be sure to ask Mr. Kreiter to be our substitute!" I hadn't felt that good since that first grader guessed I was 16 years old!

Mrs. Huss told me that things got wild on Friday. ("How much wilder could they get?" I thought.) Theodore was absent on Friday, which meant no vomiting. However, Wendell and Kathy were up to the challenge. Not only did Wendell slap Mrs. Huss on the sternum, he attempted to kick the security guards when they arrived.

Kathy spotted the beautiful, silky, page-boy hair style on the lady security guard. The guard was talking with Mrs. Huss about Wendell and not paying attention to Kathy. Kathy crept up behind her and reached for a handful of hair. Miss Martin grabbed Kathy's hand in the nick of time. Then she insisted that Kathy apologize to the lady security guard for touching her hair. Since Kathy doesn't verbalize, the ensuing grunt could have been "I'm sorry," but I suspected it was, "I'll get you next time, sweetie!"

The last educational activity on Friday was a video about an orangutan wreaking havoc in a hotel. It starred Faye Dunaway, Paul Reubens (a.k.a. Pee Wee Herman), and, of course the orangutan. Pee Wee kept the animal in a large vaudeville-style trunk. When it was released, it ripped apart the hotel and terrified the guests. As I was observing Wendell prowling around the room, trying to sneak up on staff and students alike, I whispered to Mrs. Huss, "Have you ever thought of investing in one of those trunks?"

The bell rang, and I breathed a huge end-of-week sigh of relief. As I was gathering my bang-clank equipment and coat, Mrs. Huss smiled sweetly at me and asked, "Would you please be a substitute next week as well? The permanent replacement won't be here for two more weeks." As a kid, I enjoyed watching the Saturday matinee cliffhanger serials at the Temple Theater in Bellaire, Ohio. The serial always ended with the narrator saying, "Be sure to be here next week for the next exciting chapter of The Batman!" I watched quite a few serials in my youth, but I never expected to be in one!

CHAPTER 29

Sofa, Sofa, Who's Got the Sofa?

During the second week of my CBI assignment, Reggie, the banker in the Monopoly game, "graduated" from the ranks of CBI and began attending regular classes. He had remained calm the previous week, and as far as I could tell, was a perfect gentleman. Not once had we needed to call ten men to subdue him.

Another boy came to class the day Reggie left. His name was Jody, and Mrs. Huss told the staff that he was a "big-time biter." Jody was currently living in his 3rd foster home. In his first foster home, his caregivers had kept him locked in a closet, and as a consequence, Jody walked with a permanent stoop. Teachers rarely know what children are enduring at home. Is it any wonder that so many children have trouble concentrating on the three R's? I thought, "I hope Jody bit those first foster parents good and hard!"

Jody did speak, although he had a limited vocabulary. He was fluent with both the "F" word (rhymes with duck) and the "B" word (rhymes with Mitch). We found that out when we woke him up from his afternoon nap.

There was, in addition to Kathy's bean bag chair, a sofa in the room. It, too, was in the center of Wendell's "racetrack." Jody immediately claimed exclusive rights to the sofa, so Mrs. Huss propped it up vertically to keep him from laying down on it. Bad decision. Confronted with a vertical sofa, Jody revealed his Olympic-caliber upper arm strength by slamming the sofa back to the floor. The boom registered about 6 on the Richter scale and caused everyone in the room (if not the building) to jump two feet vertically.

Jody eventually calmed down and, by the end of the day was all smiles. Before lunch, Miss Martin was whispering to Mrs. Huss about Jody and spelled his name. Jody stretched his neck up straight, raised his eyebrows, and exclaimed, "Hey! J - O - D - Y! That's my name!" In addition to biting, cussing, and body slamming sofas, Jody could spell! From then on his code name was "Star."

The sofa seemed to be the center of the universe in the CBI classroom. When one kid got up, another took his place. Considering the herculean task of dealing with Theodore, Wendell, Kathy, and now Jody, I'd be tempted to buy three more sofas and give them all sleeping pills as they entered the room.

At 11:30 A.M., I left the CBI classroom and took my sack lunch to the cafeteria. Benjamin, a boy that I had previously befriended while subbing in the Biology class joined me. A moment later Aaron spotted me and joined us. Aaron was the Ohio State fan I met on the bus to the bowling alley last week. As we were eating, someone mentioned football and Benjamin informed us that he was a Michigan fan. Aaron (bless him for this) stood up and sung - in triple fortissimo - "Oh, We don't give a damn for the whole state of Michigan ..." I shushed him and cringed. My sins had come back to haunt me.

At the close of business Wednesday, Miss Martin was leading Kathy out the door. Jody, the new kid on the block, unaware of the danger, had his back to Kathy. She reached for his hair, but Miss Martin, ever alert, pulled Kathy away from Jody in the nick of time and said, "Don't even think about it!" Kathy went home without a shock of hair; Jody went home without bald spots.

On Thursday, I felt like I had finally been accepted into "CBI's fraternity of victims." Wendell was in a sour mood. Mrs. Huss had denied him swing privileges, because he was unwilling to sit at his desk and do the morning activity. Wendell stopped in front of me, looked at me benignly, then abruptly slapped at me with his right hand. I had been on guard all week, so I was ready. I caught his right hand, and anticipated the left, which quickly followed. I looked him in the eye and said, "No - we don't hit one another!" He wandered to the other side of the room and slapped Miss Martin on the sternum! If at first you don't succeed, try, try again.

I witnessed another act of hostility by a CBI student that week. When the bell rang and it was time to escort the students to the bus pick up area, Jody decided he'd rather stay at school. Mrs. Huss and Miss Martin coaxed and cajoled him to come along with them. Instead, Jody sat down in the middle of the hallway. As I wheeled Theodore past Jody, he was showering the teachers with spit and spraying them with B and F words.

On Friday, Mrs. Huss told us about a biting incident. Several months ago, Wendell had bitten a teacher so hard that his jaws became locked like a snapping turtle's. The security guards had to come to the rescue and pry open his mouth. That story was scarier than the movie "Jaws."

Mrs. Huss followed the usual Friday afternoon routine - she dimmed the lights, slipped a DVD into the player, and showed a movie. Meanwhile Wendell was prowling around his track like a predator. He attempted to slap the teachers (perhaps hoping that security would come to the rescue and escort him home). When that produced no results, he pressed the eject button on the DVD player and stopped the show. That resulted in a volley of "No's" from Mrs. Huss, and a malevolent smile from Wendell. "Beware of a grinning Wendell," I thought.

The bell rang and Miss Martin, hoping to avoid another ugly scene in the hallway, showed Jody a flash card of a yellow school bus and tried to prepare him for the trip home. Her efforts failed to achieve the desired effect. He unleashed his entire arsenal - swearing, spitting, and scratching. To make matters worse, his bus was 40 minutes late in arriving for pickups. Poor Mrs. Huss!

When I was a teen, I worked for Fernwood Dairy on the milk truck. One of our stops was Albert's Sandwich Shoppe in Shadyside, Ohio, where I picked up a poem, entitled, "The Man Behind the Bar." Here is a portion of that poem. I have changed the "he" to "she," altered the final verse, and dedicated it to Mrs. Huss:

She deserves a hero's medal for the many lives she's saved,
And upon the roll of honor, her name should be engraved.
She deserves a lot of credit for the way she stands the strain,

For the bunk she has to swallow would drive most of us insane.
When St, Peter sees her coming, he will leave the gates ajar,
For he knows she's had her hell on earth, has this teaching superstar.

A fitting tribute to the CBI teachers of Rustic Ranch High School.

CHAPTER 30

Beware of the Double Whammy

Al Capp is regarded by some as the greatest cartoonist of all times. He drew the comic strip, "Li'l Abner" between 1934 and 1961. One of the characters in his strip was Evil-Eyed Fleegle, "whose concentrated 'whammy' stare could knock a man senseless and whose 'double whammy' could melt skyscrapers."

On an assignment at the Rustic Ranch mid high school, I served as a roving history teacher and met a young lady whose powers were on a par with Evil-Eyed Fleegle. Her name was Miss Jones. She taught history, but was also the mid high cheerleader coach. Miss Jones confessed that she was a "Military Brat," and bragged that she took no guff from any kid. The kids in her classes were the best behaved in the school.

In addition to her whammy and double whammy stares, Miss Jones's arsenal included a sergeant's bark, which, it's said, could straighten the strands on a pom-pom. During one period, she sat in the corner of the room while I taught history. It was the best behaved class I've ever taught at the mid high school. If it were possible and legal, I'd clone her and take her with me as a bouncer on all my teaching assignments.

I returned to the mid high that same week to teach eighth grade algebra and math, which, I thought, would be "right up my alley." But I was in for a surprise. The school teaches math a little differently than it did when I was in eighth grade. For example, they do partial sum division instead of long division. They also study number series and inequalities.

That day the children were to complete worksheets dealing with inequalities. After the kids started their worksheets, hands began popping up - questions! Not having time to prepare beforehand by reading the text, I looked around for the class genius, and got answers from him. The next period was "prep" (no class), so I went to the library, clutching the teacher's edition of the text, to give myself a crash course on inequalities. For the remaining six periods, when it came to inequalities, I was Mr. Infallibility.

While studying inequalities at the library, I noticed a boy opening a shoe box to examine his science project one last time before turning it in. I could see that the box contained a robotic car with a metallic frame and miniature, knobby tires. On the back of the car was a balloon, which provided the thrust. A split second after the boy opened the box, an eagle-eyed librarian was in his face, shaking her finger at him and growling, "Is that a latex balloon? Latex balloons are not allowed in school! Some people are allergic to latex! You'll have to take it outside the building!" You would have thought he smuggled the bubonic plague into the library. The poor kid looked deflated, as he left the room clutching the box. Did the librarian expect hoards of latex-sensitive students to drop dead in the halls, if he were to pass them with a balloon in a shoebox?

Later in the day, I saw four eighth grade boys standing on the stairs. Each had blown up a latex balloon and was squeezing the neck to create a high-pitch, raspy sound. They must have gotten the same latex balloon memo as the librarian. Their response was to form a banshee balloon quartet. I was tempted to tell them to please hold their rehearsals in the library.

While on the subject of balloons, I should mention that my wife prepared a craft for our second and third grade Sunday school kids that week. Each child was given two white balloons. We asked the kids to draw faces on the balloons and to tape them to a tongue depressor. The tongue depressor was to be hung from a piece of brown yarn. The two balloons represented the child and his or her best friend. We were studying the friendship between the biblical personalities David and Jonathan. Gravity was our enemy that Sunday, consequently, the finished craft hung upside down, which disturbed the kids. They would not accept my suggestion that the two balloon buddies were swinging on a trapeze.

Funny thing about balloons - they beg to be blown up. The kids, unimpressed with the original craft, cannibalized it and played with the balloons. At the morning worship service, Bev spied one of our students - Jake - sitting in the front row of church blowing up one of his balloons. Bev began praying that Jake would not release the balloon during the pastor's sermon. A white balloon, zig-zagging through the air above the heads of the worshippers might be interpreted by some of the seniors as a visitation of the Holy Spirit! It might be interpreted by the Pastor as an act of treason. Secretly, I began wishing that Jake would squeeze the neck of the balloon during the choir's anthem and be mistaken for a renegade soprano. (Jake, you are my kind of person!)

CHAPTER 31

Rats and Rights

In 1948, Columbia Pictures released the 15 chapter, action-packed Adventures of Superman, starring Kirk Alyn in the signature role. Nearly every kid was a Superman fan in the 40's and had the comic books to prove it. I sat on the edge of my seat in the Temple Theater watching Chapter 1 unfold. "Good stuff," I thought. "Just like the comics." But when, Superman said, "Up, up, and away!" my jaw dropped. The flight scene was animated, possibly by the same artists who created Mighty Mouse. The special effects were a disappointment.

Forty years later, Warner Brothers revived the legend of Superman. They produced a full-length, color movie, starring Christopher Reeve. The big question in the popcorn line was, "Will the flight scenes be realistic?" We took our seats and when Christopher went "Up, up, and away," everyone was convinced that he was airborne and had as much right to the skies as any bird or plane. The special effects were astounding.

Moviegoers witnessed a new age of realism, thanks to computer graphics and other innovative techniques. In this new age, Hollywood could make us believe that anything was possible as evidenced by movies like Star Wars, Back to the Future, Aliens, and Mary Poppins.

In high school, I watched black and white films, such as "The Lady or the Tiger." The only "special effects" in the 40's occurred when the film got stuck in the sprocket and the hot projection bulb burned the film into a brown blob before our very eyes. Today's students, however, are the beneficiaries of the new age of special effects and computer graphics. Beneficiaries and, perhaps, victims.

On an assignment at Rustic Ranch high school, I substituted for the biology teacher. In the lesson plan, she instructed me to show a video on evolution. In that movie, evolutionists presented their theories. Some things I remember from that video are: 1) the earth is 4.5 billion years old and its history may be divided into ages; 2) each age is dominated by a certain species or group of species of plant and animal life; 3) during the age of dinosaurs, some cataclysm caused the extinction of dinosaurs; 4) in the age to follow, the surviving species were little rodent-like creatures that made their homes in subterranean tunnels; and 5) all mammals, including man, have "evolved" from these underground rodents. The creators of the video used computer graphics and special effects to make the theory of evolution seem real.

I left Biology class a little depressed. The thought of hanging a picture of a rat on my wall and calling him great, great, great, great, ... grandfather was loathsome.

My next assignment was to help teach eighth grade history. Strangely enough, American history proved to be the great exterminator of evolution. The topic was the Declaration of Independence. As the class took turns reading this revered document, I was drawn to the words, "We hold these truths to be self-evident, that all men are created equal, that they are endowed by their Creator with certain unalienable rights, that among these are life, liberty, and the pursuit of happiness."

We seem to have a dichotomy here, because we are openly teaching evolution in the science classes, and we are implicitly teaching creationism in American history classes! If evolution is for real, if all life on earth is "accidental," and if mankind traces its roots to rats, then there is no

Creator. Without a Supreme Being, there is no one with authority to endow men (and women) with rights, unalienable or otherwise. Equality, life, liberty, and the pursuit of happiness are either non-existent concepts, or they apply as well to cows and polliwogs as they do to men and women!

How will educators deal with this dilemma? Should the theory of evolution prevail? Should educators remove the Declaration of Independence from our history books and discredit its authors? Or shall educators maintain the status quo and allow both evolution and creationism to continue in a state of peaceful coexistence? Those eighth grade American history teachers are surely creating problems for the high school Biology teachers!

In the Superman movie, Lois Lane asked the Man of Steel what he believed in. He replied, "Lois, I believe in truth, justice, and the American Way." The American Way is "Life , liberty, and the pursuit of happiness." Superman seems to be endorsing the existence of a Supreme Being, and if you can't believe Superman, who can you believe?

CHAPTER 32

Strike Up the Band

Music has always brought enjoyment to me. In seventh grade, I learned how to play the trumpet, and I have been playing it ever since. I've played in high school, university, and community bands and have formed musical ensembles in Cleveland, Ohio, Tucson, Arizona, and Houston, Texas.

I am a descendent of English coal miners who organized and performed in colliery bands in England. They immigrated to the U.S.A., worked in coal mines along the Ohio River, and established the

Heatherington band in Bellaire, Ohio. I love parades, halftime shows, and my favorite musical is "The Music Man."

On July 4, 1939 at Yankee Stadium, Hall of Fame first baseman Lou Gehrig gave his farewell address to baseball: "... Today I consider myself the luck- (echo: luck, luck, luck) luckiest man on the face of the earth ..." On October 30, 2008 at Rustic Ranch High School I, like Lou Gehrig, considered myself the luck- (echo: luck, luck, luck) luckiest man on the face of the earth. I had received an assignment to teach band.

I brought a baton to class. During the first two periods, I was scheduled to team teach the "Wind Symphony" and the "Concert Band." When I arrived at the rehearsal hall, the band director informed me that members of the U. S. Marine Band would be entertaining both groups, and that he and I would be listening and not directing. I thought, "Wow! I should be paying the school district today rather than accepting a wage!"

The ensemble called themselves the "Underground Brass Quintet." There were two trumpets, a trombone, a French horn, and a tuba. The bandsmen wore blue trousers with red stripes; wide, white belts with gleaming gold buckles (bearing the Marine Corps emblem); khaki colored shirts (with stripes on their sleeves and medals on their chests); and shiny black shoes. Plus they all appeared to be in excellent health and had flat tummies. I tried to suck mine in during the concert.

The Underground Brass played a variety of tunes, including a George M. Cohan Medley, The Entertainer, a Sousa March, baroque songs, and much more. They were excellent, and they did something no teacher or substitute could ever do - they commanded the kids' attention.

The first trumpet player addressed the audience: "To join a Marine Band, you take basic training, complete military combat training (MCT), and attend 6 months of concentrated music training." In MCT you learn to shoot rifles, fire grenade launchers, and do all the things marines do in combat.

The trombonist informed us that the U.S. Government employed the most professional musicians in the world. The campus recruiter informed us that the Marines were running low on musicians, so they were actively recruiting in the high schools. This really was my lucky day - I sucked in my gut and volunteered. I once fooled a first grader into thinking I was 16, but I was unable to fool the Marine recruiter!

The tuba player was a lady, originally from Chicago. In grade school she played trumpet, but when she entered high school, her band director told her that her mouth was too big to play trumpet, so he switched her to tuba. She gave us an extra wide smile and showed us 28 gleaming teeth. Her husband also plays tuba and is in the Marine Band. (Sounds like one noisy family!) She told us about her boot can ɔ experience on Paris Island. "We could only take 30 second showers and we weren't allowed to wash our hair. I have a lot of hair, so I used tons of hair spray and gel." She now wears her hair in a "sock bun," a hair style formed by wrapping the hair around a sock.

A student asked, "What famous people have you played for?" The first trumpet player replied, "I have played for Arnold Schwarzenegger and on various TV shows, such as Bob Hope's 100th birthday, the Regis Philbin show, and Wheel of Fortune. He tattled on Pat and Vanna, saying "They look really old in person and wear heavy make-up." The second trumpet player said that he had played for the President, Robin Williams, and Whoopee Goldberg. He informed us, "Robin Williams was only this tall" (indicating about 4 feet). He had also travelled to Paris, France where he performed with the Marine Band.

I tried to remember the famous people I had played for. Let's see, there was the homecoming celebration for Miss Ohio - WeeGee's beauty - at the High School football field, where I played the taps echo from behind the bleachers. I also played at astronaut David Leestma's 40th birthday party. We marched around the block imitating a New Orleans funeral dirge. The tune was "When the Saints Come Marching In." His joke birthday gift that day was an AARP magazine.

At mid day, I rushed over to the mid high school to direct the 5th period "Advanced Band." The Advanced Band consisted of seven brass musicians and seven percussionists. As I took attendance, there was a constant din of noise in the background - from the percussion section, not unlike the soundtrack of the movie "Casablanca," where Bogey and Bergman heard from afar the Germans bombing Paris.

We opened rehearsal with some warm-up scales. I finally got to use my baton. The "Rudolph Christmas Medley," was in their folder, so we tried that. Unfortunately, the woodwinds had the melody line, so all I heard were oom-pahs from the tuba and rat-a-tat offbeats from the seven drummers. One of the girls asked, "Can we put away our instruments now?" I enthusiastically replied, "Yes!" Ten minutes of class time remained. During that interval, the Advanced Band took turns trying to flip over a foot-long piece of 2x4 with their feet.

I returned to the high school to help with "Symphonic Band." The band director made some announcements, one of which was, "We won't be playing our instruments today." Then he turned the 70 students over to me and locked himself in his room. The kids were supposed to use this period as a study hall. Ha! They spread out in the band room and formed four small groups. I suddenly realized that I had become the ringmaster of a four-ring circus.

In ring 1, a dozen kids played the card game, "Spoons"; in ring 2, two dozen kids played another card game, unfamiliar to me. In ring 3, about three dozen kids were playing rock, paper, scissors. In ring 4, members of the trombone section were pushing one another around the room in wheeled chairs playing bumper cars. A handful of students actually read books or did homework. A few just sat there looking bewildered. I circulated around the room discouraging fisticuffs and lap dancing.

Toward the end of the period, the ring 3 players turned to weapons manufacturing. Using a wooden dowel and a roll of duct tape, they fashioned a flail, and they were snapping away with it. The mid high Advanced Band had its 2x4, and the high school Symphonic Band had its flail. The day ended with the students' expensive instruments in their cases and my baton in my Texas brief case. Oh well, hearing the Marine Band in the morning still made me feel like the luckiest man on the face of the earth.

Chapter 33

Advice: Avoid Advisories

The most difficult class to teach (actually, to endure) is called "Advisory." I have "served time" in Advisory at both high school and mid high. In a perfect universe, students would bring assignments to Advisory - books, worksheets, etc. - and take the initiative to study and to catch up on assignments. In my school days, we call these periods "Study Halls." In the real world it doesn't work that way. Kids sit around empty tables with dumb looks on their faces. And this, it turns out, is a best case scenario.

One resourceful high school teacher invented a check sheet to use in Advisory period. I used it. I went to each student and asked: "How many assignments do you have from your other classes?" and "What will you be working on right now?" Typical answers might be: "3/7" (meaning I have 3 assignments to complete out of my 7 classes), and "World History."

Now comes the question of credibility. Borrowing from mathematical terminology regarding inequalities, what they say is not equal to what they do. Sadly, this validates two old sayings: 1) "the best laid plans of mice and men often go awry," and 2) "you can lead a horse to water, but you can't make him drink." I left a report for the regular Advisory teacher singling out the kids who needed attitude readjustments. I wrote: "Joseph was the major epicenter of inactivity in today's Advisory period, although there were at least 2 or 3 minor epicenters."

Fortunately, I taught other classes in addition to Advisory at the mid high. During the math classes, I helped kids with their worksheets. They were computing areas of various geometrical figures. I circulated through the classroom and pointed out a "Pi R squared" here or a "one-half the altitude times the base" there. When the bell rang after math class, I felt like shouting "Hi-Ho Silver," which is what the Lone Ranger always shouted when he left town after helping the townspeople overcome a problem.

In the movie "Wizard of Oz," there is a transition from black and white to color. It occurs when Dorothy steps out of her uprooted home into Munchkin Land. She gets wide eyed and whispers to her dog, "Toto, we're not in Kansas anymore."

When I transitioned from the math class into Advisory, I had that same revelation. It was the last period of the day, it was Friday, and, although there were only 9 in the class, half were hyperactive - whip and chair cases! As I entered the room, a regular teacher was leaving. She gave me an "I know something you don't know" smile and a word of advice: "Keep them from killing one another."

I quickly surveyed the room. I saw one kid hiding in a floor to ceiling cabinet. His classmates said he spent the entire period in the cabinet the day before. One down, eight to go. Another kid produced a roll of duct tape from his backpack, taped his own legs together, and hopped around the room - a human pogo stick. I wondered what else he carried in his backpack - certainly not books, paper, or pencils. Before Advisory was over, I was having negative thoughts like, "May I please borrow your duct tape? I need to body-wrap nine individuals and mummify them until the bell rings."

A third kid had jumped up onto a table and was either doing a rain dance or shaking a scorpion out of his trousers. He did return to the floor, when I confronted him. I asked, "You do know that dancing on tables is inappropriate behavior, don't you?" The fourth hyperactive kid spent the period bending a paperclip into who knows what - perhaps a medieval instrument of torture.

Aberrant behavior on the part of mid high students shouldn't have surprised me. After all, this was the same school where one student wanted to become a male-stripper and another wanted to blow things up. The table-dancer and the male stripper seem to have a lot in common. The paper clip bender may have been working on a detonation mechanism to be used by the blower-upper of things.

In every experience there are always lessons learned. Based on my experiences in Advisory, the lessons learned were: 1) man is evolving into apes and 2) there really is a hell on earth.

CHAPTER 34

Plotting Paths

On December 1st I was asked to teach the Pathfinders class at the Rustic Ranch Mid High School. The regular teacher had travelled to Denver to see his daughter play basketball - she was on the Air Force Academy team. After the game, Denver was hit with a blizzard that left him stranded at the Denver airport. He was unable to return in time to teach the next day's classes.

The Pathfinders class is aptly named. Its goal is to help youngsters cultivate positive attitudes, develop interpersonal skills, and think about colleges and careers. In short, Pathfinders helps them find their path in life.

I showed up with my usual accoutrements - Texas brief case, badge, and whistle. The Pathfinders teacher was also coach of the girls' high school basketball team. The way the kids were looking at my whistle, I wondered if they thought I had stolen it from their teacher.

I happened to be wearing a beard - I was in a church Christmas presentation. In spite of my disguise, several of the students recognized me from an earlier visit to Pathfinders. They said, "Hey! You're the guy with the paper airplane!" On my previous visit, I had taken a box of mystery clues, including a Wheaties True-Flight airplane, a children's book - "Seeing Stars," and some Erector Set parts. I held up the box and told them that childhood hobbies often "clue us in" on what careers we should pursue. The objects in the box were my career clues. I challenged them to guess what path I took in life. Several had correctly guessed "Aerospace Engineer."

Their class assignment was to continue working on their college-of-choice posters. One lad was finished - he had chosen the University of Michigan. Outwardly I told him "Nice job!" Inwardly I gagged like any good Ohio State Buckeye would. I noticed a dozen college posters on the wall from previous semesters. The college poster would obviously have a big impact on their grade, and could make, in the long run, a big impact on their lives.

At the end of the period, I shared some ideas that James Newman introduced in his book, "Release Your Brakes." I asked them, "Have you ever heard of the term 'prison words?'" A kid in the back of the room responded, "You mean like, don't drop your soap in the shower?" I said, "I don't want to go there!"

I defined and discussed "prison words." Examples are "have to, need to, ought to, and must do." I said, "Prefacing a task with these words in your self-talk usually produces negative results." They helped me brainstorm prison word opposites, namely, "want to, look forward to, will enjoy doing, and like to."

When I was finished, I asked, "Do you have any questions or comments?" I was hoping for a "Wow! That's a new concept. I had never realized that self talk could have such an impact on what I do. From now on I'm going to carefully guard my self talk." A boy in the back smiled and raised his hand. I thought, "Here it comes!" He asked, "Where did you get your silver whistle?" So much for profound thinking with ninth graders.

I taught six Pathfinder classes that day. I tend to feel apprehensive about the last class of the day - period 7. Especially on Fridays. This was a Friday, and period 7 was upon me like a thief in the night.

The very first boy to enter the room looked like a fugitive from a dance class. He was either hyperactive or had eaten one too many candy bars. Herbie spun and pirouetted through the door, all smiles, wearing oversized shorts that I expected to drop to his ankles any minute. He was the class extrovert, and for the entire Pathfinders period, his path was a tangle. Herbie was like a bee pollinating a field of flowers, ultimately visiting all 30 classmates. Finally I ask him to please return to his hive. "Huh?" he asked. "Your desk! Your desk!"

At day's end, I wrote a report for the regular teacher, telling who was naughty and who was nice. My entry for the last period was, "Herbie," after a flamboyant, Cecil B. DeMille entry, spent the entire day in the weeds and never once found the path."

CHAPTER 35

Unfathomable Levels of Laziness

Lee Marvin won an Oscar for playing the legendary gunfighter "Kid Shelleen" in the 1965 movie, "Cat Ballou." One of my favorite scenes from that movie was the Kid's bathe and dress ceremony, where he metamorphosed from a drunken stumblebum into a black-clad, steely-eyed, two-gun cowboy. His mission: to go after the hired-gun Silvernose and avenge the murder of Cat Ballou's father.

In mid December, I was asked to substitute at Rustic Ranch Mid High School for a special education teacher. The classroom was located in a "portable" building. The last time I subbed there, one of the students had spotted a mouse that had been soiling the classroom and eluding capture. He grabbed it just as the fire alarm sounded, took it outside, and released it.

Feeling a bit festive and wondering what silver-nosed villain I might encounter in the Special Ed class, I decided to wear my black shirt, black trousers, silver necktie, black and blue plaid jacket, and gray cowboy hat.

When I stepped into the room, a wide-eyed eighth grade boy spotted me and queried, "Hey! Are you a cowboy?" I replied, "I'm a drug store cowboy." His eyes got even wider and he asked, "Do you sell drugs?" I suddenly realized that this generation has seen nothing but Walgreen-type pharmacies and has never set foot in the old fashioned drug store with soda fountains, bar stools, and "soda jerks," who could make you a Coke on the spot from syrup and seltzer.

After chuckling a few moments, I explained that a "drug-store cowboy" was a dude - a pretend cowboy - who sat on a barstool, sipped sarsaparillas, and winked at the chicks. "What is a sarsaparilla?" was the next question. "Similar to a Dr. Pepper," I replied.

That semester, the literature assignment in Special Ed was the book "Holes." "Holes" is a story about delinquent boys, sent to a camp where they had to dig large holes in the desert. The camp warden told the boys that they were digging a hole a day to build character, but she was secretly looking for buried treasure.

The teacher left me with these instructions: "Have the kids solve the hidden word puzzle. It contains vocabulary words from the book 'Holes'." There were about six kids in the classroom, and five of them started the assignment without batting an eye. Phil was the fly in the ointment. He appeared to be a forever unfocused fellow.

I sat down beside Phil and said, "Let's do this puzzle as a team. I'll find and circle one word, then it will be your turn. I'll use a brown-colored pencil; you use a green one." Phil agreed, but then the distractions began. He was clutching a small rubber snake that he repeatedly stretched and snapped. I nicely asked him to put the snake in his pocket. His eyes wondered to a classmate Annie, who was making a greeting card to send to a soldier in Iraq. He started a conversation with her. I nicely asked him to leave Annie alone and circle a word in his puzzle. A boy named C.K. came into the room to pick up worksheets for another teacher. Phil hopped up, gave C.K. a high five, and wanted to discuss current events with him. I nicely said, "Let C.K. do what he came to do. You get started on the puzzle, please."

Having been denied the rubber snake, Annie, and C.K., Phil looked at the puzzle and muttered, "How about me just telling you the word, then YOU circle it?" I gave Phil a look of utter disgust and replied, "Phil, you

Tim Kreiter

have degenerated into unfathomable levels of laziness!" Even Phil had to laugh at that diagnosis, although I had to explain to him what degenerated and unfathomable meant.

When the final bell rang, this old drug store cowboy saddled up his made-in-Detroit stallion and rode off into the sunset. Adios, Phil!

CHAPTER 36

Talent, Motivation, Attitude

Mid High students are not allowed to bring cans of spray paint to school. During the last week of every school year, security guards check backpacks and lockers to maintain a paint-free zone. School officials established this regulation to prevent the eighth and ninth graders from writing things on the walls. Kids writing things on the wall is illogical. No mid high school student reads anything posted on the wall. Why would they bother to write anything on the wall? Fellow students wouldn't even notice it! Wasted effort.

Mid high kids ought to read the things that are on the walls. While on a teaching assignment at the mid high school, I noticed the neatest poster on the wall of the science class: "Talent determines what you can do in life; Motivation determines what you are willing to do; and Attitude determines how well you will do it." If only the mid high students took these words to heart!

That day, I taught Science and Biology. The regular teacher had prepared a neat word search puzzle for the Science students, containing vocabulary words that would be on the next day's quiz. I tried doing the puzzle myself, and it took me an hour to complete. Some of the kids finished it in 15 or twenty minutes! Show offs! It was refreshing, however to witness a display of talent, motivation, and attitude in the classroom.

In second period Biology, a girl entered the room, spied me, and said, "Oh boy, a substitute! I love substitutes!" That brought a W.C. Fields story to mind. W.C. Fields, star of early 20th Century comedy films, had a bulbous nose, a blustery nature, a penchant for booze, and a disdain for dogs and kids. When asked by a reporter, "Do you like children?" W.C. replied, "It depends on how they're prepared."

The girl wasn't carrying any sharp knives or cooking implements, so I relaxed. She went on, "One of our least favorite substitutes was over 100 years old, and he fell asleep in class and drooled all over himself." I wonder how old she thought I was. The poll I took in a first grade classroom placed me between 16 and 120. How did she know that the drooling substitute was over 100? Did she check his driver's license while he was sleeping? Hoping to earn "favorite substitute status," I promised her that I wouldn't drool if I fell asleep, and I made a special effort to stay awake for those kids.

In fourth period Biology, one boisterous boy came into the classroom, laid down flat on the floor, and played dead. (Talent? Maybe. Motivation? Zero. Attitude? Bad.) Three of his ornery friends were standing around him chuckling and shifting from one foot to the other. Obviously Mr. Sleeping Beauty was testing me and trying to get the class's attention. I told his three henchmen to drag his corpse into the hall while I called the mortician. They were happy to do this! (Talent? Yes. Motivation? High. Attitude? Cooperative.) Before the body transportation degenerated into a tag team match or a hockey game, I intervened and finally got everyone seated.

During fifth period, I noticed that a young lady had set aside her word search puzzle and had unloaded the contents of her purse onto the table. I saw a compact, brushes of various sizes, lipstick, mascara, and eye pencils. I sauntered back, and as she was glamorizing her eyebrows, asked, "Are you preparing for the Miss America contest?" She blushed a little and returned her bang clank equipment to her purse, and turned her talents toward the word search. Her motivation and attitude definitely improved.

The phone rang during the final period of the day. The secretary asked me to send Tommy to the office. He left the room, then returned 10 minutes later wearing a disgusted look and clutching a school form - probably an order to report to detention hall after school. Apparently he had misbehaved in a previous class. Tommy was definitely in a dark mood - you could almost see the storm cloud hovering above his head. He sat at a back table with his arms crossed. I sashayed back to his table and ask him why he wasn't doing the word search and studying the vocabulary list. He replied, "I'm chilling out." (Talent? If only he had used it for good instead of evil. Motivation? Zilch, at present. Attitude? Off the scale - in the negative direction.)

I am supposed to leave a note for the regular teacher when I witness someone misbehaving, including "chilling out." I wrote the following words on a post-it: "Tommy has chosen to refrain from doing his assignment today. He has chosen instead to chill out. He doesn't realize that future employers are unimpressed when they see 'Chills out well' on a resume." I crept back to his desk and placed the post-it in front of him saying, "I am not going to give this note to your teacher." Ten minutes later I noticed that Tommy had started his word search assignment.

It delights a teacher when he or she is able to turn a bad situation into a good situation and see motivation go from zilch to 100 in ten seconds flat and attitude undergo an extreme makeover!

Chapter 37

Kiddie Kingdom

On a crisp Friday morning in January, I reported to the Sparkling Stars Preschool to assist Miss Tucker with her five and six year olds. My first duty of the day was to pick up the students at the bus drop-off area, next to the flagpole. When the busses began arriving, I thought they were empty! I peered in the windows, and was relieved to see little heads - way below the window line. A busload of little miniature people hopped off the bus and lined up along a wall.

The kids looked so cute as they waited in line. Each was wearing a back pack. I asked another teacher what they were carrying in them. She said "Just a folder with a few sheets of notebook paper - they are basically empty." I had seen backpacks in middle and high schools that appeared to weigh tons. Ergonomicists are really concerned that heavy backpacks will distort the kids' spines and scar them for life! A couple of helium balloons in these munchkins' backpacks would probably lift their little feet off the ground.

Preschoolers make their fashion statements by choosing snazzy backpacks and shoes. It was a day of icons for me. I saw the Incredible Hulk, Spiderman, Tinker Bell, Sleeping Beauty, Superman, and scads of other high profile characters on their backpacks, and their shoes were just as colorful and eye-grabbing. Many pairs of shoes blinked with LED's - perfect attire for a Sparkling Stars student!

Another teacher and I led the kids to the various classrooms. As they trudged along the dusty trail wearing their hooded coats and carrying their backpacks, they reminded me of miniature explorers headed for an outpost on the planet Mars. Their little backpacks looked like their life support systems, although real explorers would probably have the NASA meatball on their life support pack rather than Tinker Bell.

I led the little "explorers" into the classroom, where they shed their coats and backpacks and headed for their first activity of the day - free play time. Their favorite center was the dress-up corner. The corner of the room was like the quintessential phone booth. Kids disappeared into the corner wearing street clothes, and seconds later, emerged as Spiderman, Superman, G.I. Joe, or a plantation maiden with a wide brimmed straw hat and elbow length white gloves.

About a half hour later, Miss Tucker announced that it was clean up time. From previous gigs as a substitute, I remembered how I had to trick fifth graders to clean up the room, and how mid high students wouldn't fall for tricks or threats. But the 5 year olds were all spit and polish - they did a remarkable job cleaning the room and they did it fast. Miss Tucker asked the official class inspector to circle the room and give it her Good Housekeeping seal of approval.

It was story time next, and the kids took their assigned places on a colorful pie-shaped carpet. Little butts plopped down on yellow circles, green triangles, red squares, and purple ovals - it was a mini-amphitheater of geometrical shapes. When they were settled in, Miss Tucker read them a story entitled "Mittens." Prior to reading the story she gave each one a cardboard animal mask the size of a paper plate.

"Mittens" was a wintry story about wild animals who found a mitten lying in the snow. Each animal crawled into the mitten to get warm. As she turned the pages and read the part of the story where a particular animal - owl, or bear, or raccoon - crawled into the mitten, the kid with that particular mask crawled under a big flannel blanket at Miss Tucker's feet. When she reached "The End," eleven wiggly kids were huddled together under the blanket and giggling up a storm.

Snack time followed story time. Miss Tucker had two classes - a morning class and an afternoon class. The morning class snacked on burritos and orange juice (OJ); the afternoon class had corn dogs and OJ. There aren't many ways to eat a burrito. The kids started at one end and took them a bite at a time. Things were different with the corn dogs. Ever hear the saying "there are many ways to skin a cat"? (I must confess, in my 70+ years, I have failed to have seen even one cat being skinned.) The kids creatively consumed their corn dogs. One ate the crust first, leaving a naked frank to nibble away at. Another ate away concentric bands of crust creating a 3D barber pole effect. My favorite was the boy who ate the top half, and used the remaining half as a gavel to scatter a puddle of ketchup.

The morning class had dessert after their snacks. Little Miss Rachel was going to have a birthday the following day (Saturday), so her Mom came to class for the Friday morning snack time, bringing along a cake and Rachel's little sister, Margie, who looked like a clone of Rachel, only a foot shorter. I helped the kids eat the cake. I have a little square badge that my daughter gave me years ago. On the badge is a cake-smeared face of a boy wearing a beanie with a propeller on top. The text on the badge reads: "BORN TO EAT BIRTHDAY CAKE." I lived up to my reputation that day, except I forgot to wear a beanie.

After snack time, I was the guest of honor at a concert. The teacher asked the class to sing "The Five Frog Song," which had CD accompaniment. There was choreography too - they put one hand on their forearm to represent the frog, darted their tongues to represent the capture of the fly (glub, glub), and rubbed their tummies (yum yum) to indicate that the frog had swallowed the fly.

I read stories to both morning and afternoon classes. Both stories dealt with snow and ice and were illustrated with winter scenes. Little hands shot up throughout story telling time. Every little person had a personal snow experience to share.

The first grand finale of the day was the sequined ice ball project. Miss Tucker gave every child a balloon, a funnel, and some sequins. The 5-year olds attached the necks of their balloons to the funnels and dropped sequins down the funnels into the balloons. Miss Tucker stretched the necks of the balloons over the faucet and filled them with water, and I tied them shut. After writing their names on the balloons, we popped them into the freezer. Two days later - Monday - the Sparkling Stars preschoolers would get to admire their wintry works of art.

The second grand finale of the day was a beautiful rainbow. We had bundled up the kids for the trip home and were waiting on the buses. Suddenly it began to sprinkle and a beautiful rainbow appeared. It had the widest color bands I have ever seen - like sequins from heaven! As I watched the little ones filing into the buses, framed by the colorful rainbow, the words came to mind, "Bring the little children unto me for of such is the kingdom of heaven."

CHAPTER 38

Double Helix Delight

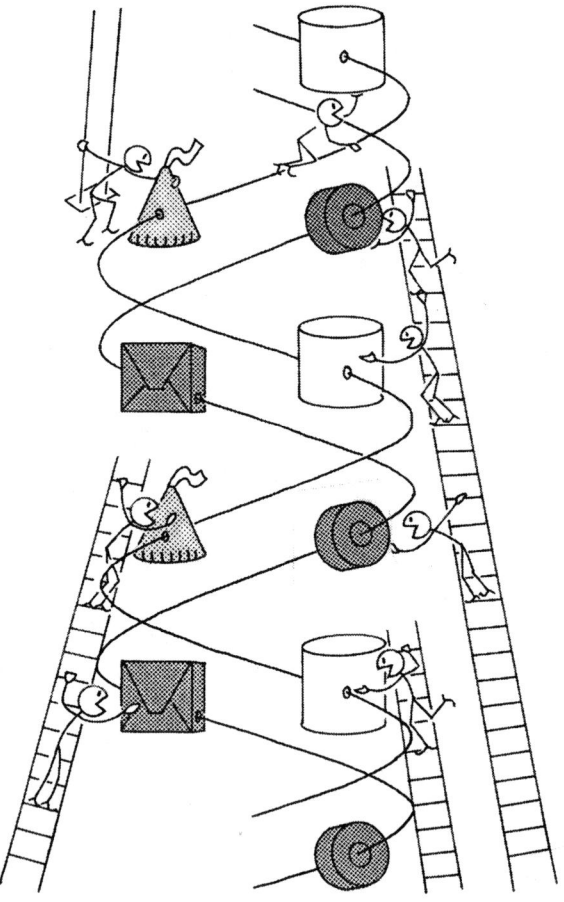

"Frogs, earthworms, and clams, oh my!" Such was the extent of the Biology course I took as a Freshman at Shadyside High School in 1950. Had someone used the letters DNA, we would probably have guessed that it was the new school slogan - Drink No Alcohol. A lot has happened in Biology classrooms over the ensuing 59 years, one of which is the study of the double helix a.k.a. DNA.

On a Friday in February I substituted for the Biology teacher at the Rustic Ranch High School. The teacher had prepared a DNA Scavenger

Hunt puzzle for the students. Quoting the instructions on the worksheet, "The DNA code is carried to the ribosome by messenger RNA; the code shown is the DNA code. You are to change the code to the m-RNA codon, and then look up each triplet codon to determine the letter the codon equals. The letters will form words, in this case, items to find in a scavenger hunt. The items must be listed and produced in the order the code dictates."

The answers were phrases. The example provided by the teacher resulted in the phrase, B-E-N-I-C-E, or, after properly spacing the letters, "BE NICE." I recalled a similar word puzzle exercise that our high school physics teacher gave us 59 years ago. (It did not involve DNA, which was yet to be discovered.) After 30 minutes of number crunching, decoding, and head scratching, one of my classmates, whom I shall refer to as "JLA," blurted out the answer - phonetically - "ABBA-DEE-GEE!" JLA had decoded all of the letters correctly, but had failed to space them properly. The desired answer was "A BAD EGG," which perfectly described most of us pupils.

The Biology teacher had assigned some very creative projects during the semester. I scanned the room and found two that were especially intriguing. For their first project, students had made models of the double helix and had placed them on display atop the room-length counter, in the back of the classroom.

I had to chuckle at the variety of materials the students had chosen to construct their models. Fifty-nine years ago, if we had to build such a complicated model, we would have probably used Tinker Toys. But 21st century Biology students think outside the box. They used: pipe-cleaners, jelly beans, gumdrops, licorice sticks, beads, mini-marshmallows, Fruit Loops, popsicle sticks, Styrofoam balls, and chunks of Mexican candy. The beauty of it all was, after the teacher had finished grading the projects, the kids could eat their double helixes.

One of my favorites was inedible - the student had made it with heavy gage wire, metal brackets, and hexagonal nuts. Each component was painted the appropriate color to represent DNA coding, and the assembly was mounted on a wooden frame. I checked to see who submitted this masterpiece. His name was Mack, and he was in the 5th period class.

I noticed a pile of crumbled, red pipe cleaner segments on the back table. I wondered if this had originally been a double helix project that had gone bad. Perhaps the student had used dog biscuits as DNA components and his dog had eaten the model on the way to school. (A perfect excuse for not turning in your project - the dog ate it.)

The second project was a study of heredity. Each kid had to select a hypothetical father and mother, ascribe traits to each parent - complexion, eye shape and color, hair texture and color, and other physical characteristics - then, by applying the theory of dominant and recessive genes (and an occasional toss of the coin) determine the probable traits of the offspring and draw their portraits on an 8-1/2 by 11 inch sheet of paper. A rogue's gallery of faces lined the walls of the Biology lab. If these portraits were accurate renditions, I believe laws should be passed to prevent some of these hypothetical couples from mating!

The previous week, I had taught at the Sparkling Stars preschool and had noticed that preschoolers make their fashion statements with their choice of backpacks and shoes. On the high school campus, students often make their fashion statements by choice of hairstyles. In my Biology classes, four students had outstanding, if not outrageous hairstyles. I imagined these four as finalists, vying for a Weird Hairdo trophy. "Best Home Videos," eat your heart out!

Of the 5 periods I taught, four of them had contestants. In Period 2, a boy named Romulus had the scariest hairdo I've ever seen. His head was shaved and on the top were what appeared to be four black, oily tarantulas, possibly sucking out his brains, or at least tapping into his cerebellum and controlling him a la Invasion of the Body Snatchers! He sat there as calm and composed as if everyone in the world wore black, oily tarantulas on their heads.

In Period 3, a girl named Bethany glided into the room with her straight hair wafting in the breeze. It was shoulder length and uneven, as if it had been mercilessly butchered by either an angry brother or a student barber at a discount beauty shop. Streaks of fluorescent pink color highlighted the mousy brown strands. As an accessory, she wore a black, frilly tutu over her jeans.

Contestant number 3 was a boy named Sam, who had a full head of hair that he had colored gray. He had slicked it down with something - possibly a product that I had heard advertised on the radio half a century ago (*You'd better get Wildroot Cream Oil, Charlie - it keeps your hair in trim*, or *Brylcreem, a little dab'll do you, Brylcreem, you'll look so debonair*, or *It's clear, it's clean, it's Vaseline hair tonic for your hair!*). If not a commercial hair product, then perhaps his natural oils (ugh!). This mature looking lad, in need of an oil change, however, was the only person that period to complete his DNA Scavenger Hunt. Underneath that oily gray scalp was some impressive gray matter.

Contestant number 4 was Mack, who had shaved his entire head, except for a tiny seam of blond hair down the center, separating left brain from right brain. It wasn't a bushy Mohawk like a pro wrestler, but thin and wispy like dandelion blossoms. Mack, however was the student who had built the heavy-duty, wood and metal, double helix model, so if he failed to win the Weird Hairdo trophy, he was almost certain to win the double helix model contest.

As I've said before, every experience carries with it a "lessons learned." My day at the Biology lab made me realize that 1) 21st century students have a much larger body of knowledge to process than their grandparents did; 2) 21st century teachers are doing a remarkable job and making learning fun through the use of creative projects; and 3) a tarantula hairdo will win the Weird Hairdo trophy every time.

CHAPTER 39

Bonnie's Band

One of my very first substitute teaching jobs - over a year ago - was at the Sparkling Stars Preschool. I worked with an aide named Miss Bonnie. Imagine my surprise to return and discover that we would again be working together. Miss Bonnie was a grandmother, came from Brooklyn (and had the accent to prove it), and had the demeanor of a drill sergeant. She knew how to keep 5-year olds in line!

Sparkling Stars Preschool is much more than a babysitting service. Young minds are really shaped there. Teachers keep exhaustive records of their progress and document what the kids say and what they're taught. These records are entered into the computers and used to track kids through high school graduation. They are hoping to develop "metrics" that will improve the educational process.

A shy little boy came in the door and sat down quietly in the corner. I went over, kneeled down, and said "Good morning, my name is Mister Tim. I am so happy to be your teacher today. What is your name?" He replied, "My name is Arthur, and my Dad is a Ninja."

I asked him to tell me more. Arthur continued, "My Dad wears a black uniform and has a sharp sword that he carries on his back." I said "Wow!" (and meant it.) Then he said, "My Mom is going to another planet - it's called DC." (I had a sarcastic thought at that point, about the political goings-on in DC, and how it could well be defined as another planet.) Arthur finished, "There are no thorns in DC - just grass, flowers, and apple trees."

A boy named Hal, who was wearing a brand new camouflage-colored hooded jacket, walked over, joined the conversation, and said, "My Dad works on a submarine!" (I found that a little hard to believe since the Rustic Ranch school district is in the middle of a desert.) I inquired, "What does he do on the submarine?" Hal replied, "I think he launches rockets from under the water." That drew another "Wow!" from me.

Miss Bonnie overheard their conversations and scurried to the desk for paper and pencil. Mary's Dad sold hand-made jewelry. Andy's Dad was a policemen and "arrested bad guys." Tammy's father was in jail - "He broke the law." (Did Andy's dad put him there?) Richard's Dad "Made money and sent it to banks." (Was he a counterfeiter?) Miss Bonnie, never questioning their veracity, dutifully recorded these revelations and inserted them into the school's database.

At recess, the kids donned their jackets and went outside to the playground. The entire play area was carpeted with shredded rubber, providing a soft safe place to romp around. One little girl, apparently an object of worship to the little boys, led four of the little lads around the perimeter of the play area. They were crawling on all fours. I asked her what she was doing. She replied, "Walking my animals." I said, "Oh, you have four dogs?" One of the "animals" corrected me: "I am a dragon!" So it was three dogs and a dragon. One of the dogs pushed out his lips and said, "And I smoke!" Make that one dragon, and three dogs, one of whom smoked.

I brought my trumpet with me to school. After morning recess, Miss Bonnie sat the kids on the floor and invited me to show them my trumpet and to play them some songs, which I gladly did. Word got around, and when the afternoon kids arrived, I was invited to present an outdoor concert to the entire student body. The classes started arriving and the kids and their teachers filled the stone amphitheater. The Principal, Mrs. Howard welcomed me and introduced me to the children. About 50 feet away some workmen were using a Skilsaw to trim the roof of an adobe playhouse. Mrs. Howard spoke to the workmen, and asked them to please put away their saw during the concert - we didn't need Skilsaw accompaniment.

I explained how a trumpet was constructed - how the tubes were folded to reduce the length and how valves were pressed to change the length and tone of the instrument. I blew my police whistle to illustrate how some instruments, such as clarinets, flutes, and saxophones are played. Then I told them that brass instruments were played by making a buzzing sound with the lips. I taught them how to buzz. I raised the mouthpiece and buzzed into it. Then I inserted the mouthpiece into the trumpet and played a middle C. They *oohed* and *aahed* at the sound.

I played two bugle calls for them. "REVEILLE," I said, "is the tune buglers play to wake up soldiers in the morning." As I played, Miss Bonnie sang (in a brassy Brooklyn voice that was ever so slightly off key), "I can't get 'em up, I can't get 'em up, ..." Then I played "TAPS," telling them this was the tune buglers played to tell the soldiers to fall asleep. Miss Bonnie sang, "Go to sleep; go to sleep; go to sleep, go to sleep, go to sleep,.. ."

The kids had just celebrated Presidents Day, so I asked them if they knew that Presidents have a special song. Some claimed they knew. I played "Hail to the Chief" and got a big round of applause.

Miss Bonnie had brought a box of rhythm instruments with her, and she distributed them to about two dozen kids. Then she ordered everyone to stand up and informed them that they would march while Mr. Tim played the trumpet. I gave my best rendition of the Stars and Stripes Forever and the Buckeye Battle Cry. Leading the parade was Miss Bonnie, beating a plastic drum and giving a first-rate impersonation of Robert Preston, from the closing scene of "The Music Man," where he pranced and weaved out of the River City high school auditorium, leading the River City Boys Band.

The last activity of the day was free play. A marvelous thing happened during free play. Five little 5-year olds created a work of art every bit, if not more impressive than the double helix DNA models that the high school biology students had created. Julie, Brent, Phoebe, Kay, and Tina worked as a team to create a colorful train from geometric shapes. The base was a string of yellow hexagons, 40 pieces long. On each yellow hexagon, they had carefully placed a red trapezoid, then a blue rhombus, and finally a green equilateral triangle. It was so attractive and colorful, Miss Bonnie borrowed a digital camera from a neighboring teacher and snapped a picture.

When you assemble a dozen 5 year olds and give them blocks or Leggos, you expect chaos and an "every man for himself" atmosphere. At Sparkling Stars, however, I witnessed planning, skillful execution, and cooperation on the part of the design team and respect from the non-participants. Congratulations, teachers of Sparkling Stars - you must be doing something right!

At day's end I walked the kids to bus pickup. Three buses serviced the school. One was late. A substitute driver finally arrived. He was wearing a cowboy hat. The first kid to enter the bus looked at him, then looked back at me, and said, "Do we have to drive home with a cowboy?!"

Oh, by the way, when Hal's Dad came to pick him up, I noticed that he was NOT wearing a naval uniform. I greeted him and asked, "Do you really work on a submarine?" He laughed hysterically, grabbed Hal's hand and chuckled all the way to the parking lot. I wondered how many other kids had fed me fantasies about their Dads and Moms. Today's data entries are sure going to befuddle Bonnie's computer records!

CHAPTER 40

Promises, Promises

Not all of the brilliant-minded people in the southwest end up at the Los Alamos labs, delving into the world of quantum physics. One - Mrs. LaCosta - became a first grade teacher within the Rustic Ranch School District. She left me the most elaborate and detailed six-page lesson plan I have ever had the privilege of using. She had also systematically laid out the associated books and teaching supplies on custom shelves that she had made from six foot sections of aluminum rain gutters. Mrs. LaCosta was a remarkable teacher.

If you think that 21st century first graders spend their days coloring inside the lines and printing with fat lead pencils on yellow lined tablets, you are mistaken. Mrs. LaCosta's kids adhered to a carefully-planned routine that included creative writing, mathematics, music, and computer training.

We opened the day with, "I pledge allegiance to the flag, of the United States of America." Then we turned our eyes from the American flag to a large poster mounted on the wall. At the top of the poster was printed the title, "OUR PROMISE." The kids recited the first grade promise which was:

> *"When we care about each other, we share what we have, listen carefully, help each other learn, take turns, and have fun together. We understand that we all make mistakes, that we stand up for ourselves and others, and when someone asks us to stop, we stop. This is who we are even when no one is watching."*

I thought, "Wow! Mrs. LaCosta has created a classroom full of perfect angels!" But as the day wore on, I realized that "Our Promise" was a work in progress. It brought to mind a book my own children used to read, entitled "Nobody Is Perfeck." The story was about a little boy named Peter Perfect who

> *Always sat up straight*
> *Was never absent or late*
> *Was always helpful*
> *Never daydreamed*
> *Came to class prepared - with a sharp pencil*
> *Never giggled in class*
> *Never slurped his milk*
> *Never talked with his mouth full*
> *Never stuck out his tongue*
> *Never interrupted when someone else was talking*
> *Never dropped crumbs*
> *Always scrubbed behind his ears*
> *Slept without a nightlight*

On the final page of "Nobody Is Perfeck," appeared the words, "If only you were real, Peter Perfect," and a picture of a little robot boy with a giant wind-up key emerging from his back!

In a "perfeck" classroom, children would remain in their chairs while the teacher presented the lesson. Mrs. LaCosta's little people were in orbit around me all day. I felt like the planet Jupiter (complete with equatorial bulge) with an entourage of many little moons encircling me. They say necessity is the mother of invention, and in my mind I was inventing velcro cushions for the first graders. I visualized a fuzzy patch sewed to the seats of their pants and a Velcro pad glued to the seats of their chairs. The chairs should probably be bolted to the floor, otherwise the little orbiting moons would have chairs protruding from them.

Every room has a class cop, and Carlos was ours. He was the innermost orbiting planet, and he was perpetually in my ear, whispering advice or tattling about classmates: "Alan is hitting Clark; Lisa is out of her chair (they all were out of their chairs); Sarah is sleeping in the corner; Michael just left the room; Wesley is teasing Samantha; etc., etc., etc."

I took my break Monday morning after I dropped the children off at the computer lab. Mrs. LaCosta had given them a writing assignment to commemorate their 100th day of school, which occurred on Tuesday. The media of choice in the 20th century was paper and pencil. These first graders were using computers! Kids wrote in a text box the sentence, "If I had 100 dollars, I would buy ..." (They had to fill in the blank.) Then they used the graphics tool to make a picture. I looked over their shoulders to see what they'd buy if they had a hundred dollars. I saw "100 snakes, 100 pieces of candy, 100 cats, 100 snails, 100 kittens" - things every 21st century first grader needs.

During the reading session, kids were supposed to sit on the carpet in front of me. Each had a name tag taped to the floor (non-Velcro variety). The tag directly in front of me was unoccupied. Sarah was missing. I saw Sarah standing in the back of the room holding a giant wad of dripping paper towels. By the looks of things, the school water tower had ruptured, and Sarah was mopping it up. Later, we discovered that two bottled waters had tipped over near Sarah's desk.

After reading came lunch time. I checked the lesson plans and found that teachers stay with their kids at the cafeteria until they've finished eating. We scurried single file down the hall to the cafeteria. Stepping through the door to the cafeteria was like entering a new world, and not necessarily a better one. The noise level in an elementary school cafeteria lies somewhere between the rumble of the New York subway and the roar of the Los Angeles Coliseum when the home team scores a touchdown.

I had a close call in the cafeteria. It was in the slip, trip, and fall category. At Disneyland there is an armada of workers who scour the grounds with whisk brooms and dustpans. Their job - keep the walkways free of debris. You rarely see a peanut shell or a gum wrapper beneath your feet at the Magic Kingdom. Contrast that to school cafeterias. As I arose from my seat and was preparing to leave, Elaine grabbed my hand and said, "Stop! Look!" I glanced at the floor near my shoe. I had nearly stepped on a mound of macaroni and cheese. I believe that more macaroni winds up on the cafeteria floor than in the mouths of the kiddy customers. But, hey - No Cafeteria Is "Perfeck"!

That afternoon I got another break. Miss Baker, the librarian visited our class accompanied by a young Japanese lady, who was an expert on origami. The two of them taught our children how to create origami objects of art. The kids made a cat, a bird, and a butterfly. The air was filled with flying cats, birds, and butterflies. There is an organization - "The Confederate Air Force" - that tours the country and reenacts World War II air battles. What we had in Mrs. LaCosta's first grade classroom was a paper Pearl Harbor reenactment.

Like the residents of Hawaii on December 7, 1941, the librarian, the Japanese origami consultant, and I were feeling a bit frazzled after the origami experience. The final bell was scheduled to ring at 4:00 P.M. I looked at the clock, and it was only 3:45! It seemed as though we were trapped in a cruel Einstein time dilation, where seconds stretched into hours - maybe days.

The bell did finally ring. The students had enough energy to break the "no running in the halls" rule. I moved considerably slower. As I ambled down the hall, exhaling the word, "Phew!" several regular teachers bid me good day, saying, "Well, I see you made it." I wondered how many of my predecessors didn't. And by the way, Mrs. LaCosta, you neglected to include on your detailed lesson plan, what the teacher should do to rejuvenate himself after the bell rings.

CHAPTER 41

Potties, Potties

Tuesday, February 3rd was the first graders' 100th day of school. It was my second day with them - it only seemed like the 100th. Each kid brought a zip lock bag of 100 treats - m&m's, candy corn, Cheerios, mini marshmallows, candy hearts, graham bears, raisins, Boston baked beans, etc. Later that day we mixed them all in one big bowl and gave each child a cupful of 100th day treats.

First grade teachers read a lot of stories during the week. In a "perfeck" world, first grade students would do a lot of listening. Story

Adventures of a Substitute Teacher

time, however, wasn't so much a time for listening as it was for drinking and peeing. Their teacher, Mrs. LaCosta had instituted sign language for the kids to use when a certain need arose. Pointing to the throat meant, "I'm dry or my throat is sore. May I go get a drink of water?" Pointing the index finger to the ceiling meant, "I have to go to the potty and do number 1." Palm forward with the thumb between the first and second finger meant, "I have to go to the potty and do number 2." The latter was a little too graphic, I thought.

Proudly remembering my Velco solution to the "keep kids seated" problem, I racked my engineering brain for a solution to the "I want a drink" and "I've got to pee (or poo)" problems. The short term solution was to march the entire column of parched peanuts to the fountain en mass, with a stop at the restrooms during the return trip. I did that, but no sooner had we gotten back to our room, two or three kids began pointing to their throats again! In the words of Charlie Brown, "Aaaaaarrrrrgggghhhh!!"

Many kids brought bottled water to class. Many others didn't. Those that did often spilled it. Ergo, the widespread throat pointing. One long term solution to "thirstus interruptus" might be a community seltzer bottle. When a child points to his or her throat, teacher would respond with a "Say Ah!" and then squirt a jet of water into the open mouth, like a mother bird dispensing worms to her young in the nest.

The solution to the "I've got to go - either number one or number two" problem was more complicated, and took considerably more thought. After cogitating on the problem for two days, the answer suddenly hit me. Install little flush toilets in the classroom. Spread them out in a fan shaped pattern creating a little amphitheater of potties. This would be their regular seating arrangement during story time. The teacher, of course, would sit at the apex of the amphitheater with her book and seltzer bottle - a "perfeck" holistic solution!

That Tuesday morning, I referred to my six-page lesson plan and saw that our class was scheduled to report to the music room for singing and rhythm instrument playing. I dropped them off for 45 minutes of music making (suspecting that it would consist of 50% music, 25% trips to the fountain, and 25% trips to the potty). I also noticed that I had recess duty immediately after music. After picking them up at the music room, I escorted them to the playground and watched them run, play, toss balls, and chase one another. Cory asked me if I'd play tag with him and two other boys. I begged off and said no, using my age as an excuse. Cory replied, "OK, then, could you be base?"

When the bell rang, I shook the dust off my shoes, and we all returned to the classroom for craft time. In keeping with the 100th day, Mrs. LaCosta had prepared individual craft kits for the kids. Each kit contained 100 Apple Jacks (apple flavored cereal shaped like Cheerios) and about two feet of yarn. The kids sat down and made their necklaces. Yarn tends to get fuzzy on the end when you poke it through Apple Jacks, creating a problem that required yet another engineering solution. I trimmed the ends of the yarn and wrapped scotch tape around the ends. Now they had a "shoelace," which fit nicely through the cereal loops. Half of the class wore their necklaces to lunch.

During the lunch period, three girls crowded in next to me. They apparently 1) liked me, 2) were curious and wanted to see what was in my lunch bag, or 3) wanted to bum food. Elaine sat directly across from me wearing her Apple Jacks necklace. I had to laugh when I looked at Michael, who was sitting next to her. There were only two Apple Jacks left on the yarn. He gave me a big smile, revealing two missing upper teeth, proving that Apple Jacks may be either chewed or gummed. Oh, by the way, I did give samples of my lunch to my female admirers - I shared my celery, tangerine, and sugar wafer cookies.

Later in the afternoon, while we were eating the mixture of 100 treats, I told the class the story of my daughter Kimberly. When Kimmy was in first grade, she took two quarters to school. Only they never got to school, because she stopped at a Mom and Pop candy store along the way and bought 50 pieces of bubble gum. She hid them in her desk. Her teacher caught her chewing gum and ordered her to spit it out. Kimmy secretly reloaded, and the next time teacher gave her the eagle eye, Kimmy slipped the gum from her mouth and hid it in her belly button (obviously an "innie"). When she got home, she cried to her Mom that her belly hurt. Her Mom raised her skirt and slip and discovered why. Bubble gum was sticking to her slip and skirt and pulling on her skin. The class loved this story. Being inspired, Wyatt hid an M&M in his belly button and proudly showed it to the class. Later that day, by popular demand, I retold the bubble gum story.

We finished the 100th day celebration with gusto. Lacking a seltzer bottle, I improvised. Before me sat an audience of little mouths. I said, "Say, Ah," and pitched mini-marshmallows onto the tongues of eager receivers. As some anonymous guru once said, in the not-so-desirable, passive voice, "A good time was had by all."

CHAPTER 42

Marshmallow Toes

The regular teacher, Mrs. LaCosta, attended teacher training on Monday, Tuesday, Thursday, and Friday, but she was back at the helm on Wednesday, and I got a day's rest. Thursday morning, I reported for duty, and again, the lesson plans had been placed on the desk and the books and supplies were arranged on the shelves. There is a fairy tale about the Elves and the Shoemaker. A certain elderly shoemaker was in desperate need of help. His business was on the verge of collapsing. Elves took pity on him, and, while he slept, the elves came into his shop, cut leather shoe parts, sewed the pieces together, and polished the shoes to a glossy shine. When the shoemaker woke up, he found his store filled with dozens of pairs of shiny new shoes, and suddenly he was prosperous! The shoemaker never saw the elves. I was the shoemaker in this metaphor.

If I remember my first grade years accurately, stories always began with "Once upon a time" and finished with "The End." Furthermore, we merely read the stories - usually Dick and Jane - we never wrote them. Mrs. LaCosta challenged her class to write stories, and she was teaching them writing techniques, in particular, how to plan the opening line of a story and how to write its conclusion. On Thursday, they were to focus on the opening line of a story and to design it to grab the reader's attention.

We used the poem "Little Bo Peep" as a stepping off point. I told them, "No one knows what Bo Peep was doing when she lost her sheep. Your job is to tell what she was doing when the sheep disappeared and to write that down as the opening line of your story." Here are some of their opening lines:

> *Little Bo Peep was chewing gum when she lost her sheep.*
> *Little Bo Peep was washing her hair when she lost her sheep.*
> *Little Bo Peep was vacuuming when she lost her sheep.*
> *Little Bo Peep was picking berries when she lost her sheep.*
> *Little Bo Peep was being abducted by aliens when she lost her sheep.*

While the kids were composing their opening lines, I played (as instructed) Mrs. LaCosta's "Writing" CD - soft music to create the proper mood for budding authors.

Just before recess, Samantha wanted permission to go get a drink. Up until then, I had always given a nod of approval whenever anyone pointed to their throat, raised an index finger, or showed me the palm of their hand. But on this occasion, the class was scheduled to leave for Physical Education in two minutes. I said, "No. Let's wait and get our drinks on the way to PE." Samantha gave me a simultaneous frown, pucker, and pout. Then she stood up, planted her feet, and made a little speech, "My Mom says I need to drink lots of water while I'm at school so I don't get dehydrated!" She stomped to the corner and sulked for two minutes.

I marched the troops down the hall and deposited them in the gym. "Coach," I told the PE teacher, "they are all yours!" When I returned 45 minutes later, every one of them had a jump rope. This was Heart Health Month, and the school gave each child a jump rope to promote regular exercising.

There are many things a child can do with a jump rope (besides jumping). The first graders held their jump ropes like Indiana Jones held his bullwhip. I punctuated the march back to the classroom with commands like, "OK, Nathan, roll up that jump rope and carry it! Scott, don't trip George with your jump rope!" After arriving in the room, Michael strung his jump rope between desks and tripped Lisa. I grabbed as many ropes as I could see, coiled them, taped them shut, and asked the kids put them in their back packs.

The Thursday vocabulary assignment was "rainbow letters." Each child picked three different colored stacking pens and wrote out the vocabulary words, alternating the colors of the letters. The kids snapped several pens together, so that they were printing with 12 inch long pens. Others, thinking, "I can top that," snapped four together, then five. Some stopped writing altogether and began constructing pipelines on the floor. They ended the vocabulary session with a stacking pen sword fight. If only they had used their jump ropes and stacking pens for good instead of evil.

Thursday, I noticed a poem on the wall above the door. I hadn't noticed it on Monday and Tuesday. I should have - it was on page 3 of the lesson plan. The students were supposed to read the poem before leaving the classroom. The title was "Marshmallow Toes." It went like this:

> *Walking through the hallway,*
> *Everyone quietly goes,*
> *Being respectful all the way,*
> *Walking on marshmallow toes.*

Nice thought! In the real world, my first graders walked on Buffalo hooves, and a trip through the hall was more like a stampede! From then on, my hall talk was, "Marshmallow toes! Marshmallow toes!"

When the dismissal bell rang Thursday afternoon, the teacher from across the hall came into my room, probably to hold a cold mirror under my nose. I told her I was OK, just worn to a frazzle. She, on the other hand looked as perky as the Tournament of Roses Queen. She claimed she felt tired, too, but I think she was just trying to cheer me up.

In the movie, "Night at the Museum," Ben Stiller staggered out of the museum at the end of his shift looking drained, wilted, and frazzled. He had just spent the night battling Lilliputian armies, avoiding wild lions and elephants, outrunning a berserk dinosaur, warding off Ghengis Khan and the Mongol hoard, and trying to outwit crazy monkeys. You can see where I'm going with this.

CHAPTER 43

Beach Therapy

On the last day of a four day assignment at the Rustic Ranch Elementary School, Ms. Adamson, the school counselor was the guest teacher. She gave the first graders a lesson on anger management. They all sat on the carpet in their assigned places and did what was expected of them - they squirmed and wiggled. Ms. A. told them a story about two boys at the water fountain. One boy pushed and shoved the other boy out of line, so he could be first at the fountain. The boy that got shoved was angry, but he controlled his anger. The counselor asked the class,

"What do you think the boy who was shoved did to control his anger?" They replied:

He got away from the other boy
He told himself to stay calm
He counted to ten

Ms. A. complimented them, "Very good, children. Now let me show you another way to calm down when you are upset." She continued, "Imagine you are at the beach. You are laying down on the warm sand. Your eyes are closed and you feel a warm breeze blowing over you. How do you feel?" They replied:

Warm and safe
Good
Itchy
I want a drink
I have to use the restroom

I sat on the floor with them - a special concession allowed me by Ms. A. Three kids immediately leaned against me, imagining me to be a warm sand dune. The class remained motionless for about 5 minutes, letting their rage, anger, and anxieties flow into the warm sand. Ms. A. left the classroom smiling, confidant that at least a part of the world was now under control.

During the science lesson, we discussed the states of matter - gas, liquid, solid. Then we did worksheets, which had pictures of tea pouring from a pitcher, an ice cube, popcorn, a bubble, and several other items. They had to print gas, solid, or liquid underneath each picture. We finished by having a snack - potato chips (solid) and Kool-Aid (liquid). I had balloons for them, which represented the gaseous state of matter, but I decided to postpone that part of the demo until 5 minutes before the final bell. I wasn't born yesterday (four days ago, yes).

Their teacher Mrs. LaCosta had been at a conference all week, so I sat them down on the infamous carpet and asked them to tell me what they thought she was studying at the conference. Here are some of their replies:

She is training for Math.
She is training to learn how us to line us up.
She is training to be a better teacher (very generic answer).
She is learning how to count to 600.
She is learning how to count beyond 600 - maybe to 7,000.

> *She is getting trained to spell.*
> *She is learning how to count to pi. (Where did a first grader learn about pi?)*
> *She is learning how to become a Seltzer bottle marksman. (That was mine.)*

Family show and tell was the grand finale of the week. Every week a different child gets to tell his or her story. On Monday, Nathan had brought a stack of family photos, which Mrs. LaCosta had stick-pinned to a 3 foot square cork board. On Friday afternoon, Nathan took center stage and described the photos on the cork board.

Nathan's grandmother visited us on Friday. She told me that Nathan's great uncle was Jim Thorpe, famous college athlete and Olympic gold-medal winner. Nathan was also a descendent of the native American Chief Tecumseh and another renown Seminole Chief from Oklahoma. Nathan's grandmother brought an empty Wheaties box. On the front was a picture of Jim Thorpe in his Carlyle College football uniform. She also brought a 10 by 12 glossy picture of Jim when he was about 60 years old.

Nathan told the class about himself and his family. The earliest photo taken of Nathan was an ultrasound picture of himself. He told us about the rest of his family, including his dog. Kids were allowed to raise their hands and ask him questions after he had finished. All of their questions were about his dog. Nobody in first grade had ever heard of Jim Thorpe nor were they impressed by Mr. Thorpe's picture on the Wheaties box.

I was impressed by his famous ancestor. I spoke to Nathan's grandmother and gave her a "data dump" on what I knew about Jim Thorpe. She was surprised at my vast knowledge of Mr. Thorpe, and she asked, "How do you know so much about Jim Thorpe?" I confessed that I had seen the 1950 biography starring Burt Lancaster.

It was 3:55 P.M. so I bribed the kids into to putting on their jackets and backpacks, by promising them balloons. "What possible mischief could they perpetrate in 5 minutes?" I thought. They blew up the balloons and released them. (Shades of origami day!) Some blew them up and squeezed the neck, making eerie, shrill noises (I'm afraid I taught them that trick earlier in the afternoon.) The "savers" blew theirs up and asked me to knot the end (a messy, spitty job, I might add), and then they head butted them into the air. The place looked like the Albuquerque Balloon Fiesta.

The bell rang and I walked them out to the bus and car pickup area. Samantha had two big pink balloons in her hands. She met her older brother at the flagpole, and they waited together for the minibus along with six other children. I observed the usual pushing and shoving, and then I heard a loud "POP!" One of Samantha's balloons had entered oblivion. She blamed her brother, got teary eyed, and began venting her anger on him. It degenerated into a two-person shouting match. The brother got upset and denied bursting sister's balloon! At the peak of the altercation, the bus pulled in and the kids began climbing the steps. Samantha was wailing. I called to her: "Samantha, you are laying on a warm sandy beach, a warm salty breeze is blowing, ..."

Actually, I didn't do this, but I thought about it. My mission now was to go home for the weekend and look for a warm sandy beach.

Chapter 44

Things Failed to Add Up

In baseball, they call them "designated hitters." In the Rustic Ranch School District, they call them "Floating Subs" (FS). Floating Subs travel from classroom to classroom throughout the day. For example, teacher A leaves her classroom during period 1 for a parent teacher conference, and the FS covers for her. Teacher B leaves her classroom during period 2 for a parent teacher conference, and the same FS covers for her, and so on. Like baseball, sometimes the floating sub hits a home run during the period; sometimes he strikes out.

Adventures of a Substitute Teacher

Floating subs often find themselves in a logistics situation similar to that of an air traveler. Arrive at gate A48, depart from gate A1. And time is critical. In the floating sub assignment I accepted, I had 5 minutes to get from the period 1 class to the period 2 class, and the rooms were on opposite sides of the school. Unfortunately, they don't provide the little electric cars.

I was about 20 minutes early for my period 1 class. A little girl named Sydney came into the room before the others. She smiled, introduced herself, and said she knew everything that went on in the class room and that she would like to help me. Wow! There is an expression, "You'll never get a second chance to make a first impression." Sydney made a great first impression.

The teacher left two worksheets - one for Language Arts (LA), the other for Math. After the customary roll call, lunch count (fabulous choice of food), and posting of date and day of week, I began to distribute the Language Arts worksheets (with help from Sydney and Morris). Suddenly the fire alarm sounded. There is a saying that a manager's job is that of moving from one interruption to another. The same can be said of teachers.

All went well after the first graders returned to the class room. We completed both the LA and the Math worksheets before I had to race off to the far corners of the earth and sub for a third grade teacher. The third grade teacher had left instructions for me to escort the third graders to the computer lab and act as consultant while the boys studied math and the girls studied reading. I was impressed with the computer lab. The computers were new and of the same quality as those I used at Johnson Space Center before retiring. The school provided interactive computer based training (CBT) modules to present the lesson material. In my lifetime, I have seen lesson technology leap from the medium of yellow chalk on black slate boards to state-of-the-art computers. It made me feel like a 70 year-old eraser duster.

My next task for the morning - teaching another first grade class - took me back to "the other side of the airport," and I had to hustle to be on time. These first graders were studying two of the most vital topics known to man: 1) how to tell time, and 2) how to make change.

From their worksheets, they learned: a fifty cent piece is the equivalent of two quarters; you may pay for an 85 cent box of crayons with either 8 dimes and a nickel, or three quarters and a dime. The kids completed their worksheets and lined up for their trip to the cafeteria. As they marched off to lunch, I overheard Jenny say, "Hey, I lost a quarter." Jeff said, "I lost two quarters!" "That would be fifty cents, Jeff," I said.

I had time for a quick lunch, so I headed for the teachers' lounge and visited the adjacent men's staff room. When I stepped into this 6 foot by

7 foot room, I was dazzled. My first thought was, "Did Frank Lloyd Wright design this rest room?" Pale green drapes and a white curtain adorned one wall suggesting the presence of a picture window. The other walls were adorned with western accessories, such as a sombrero, a Navajo rug, and a miniature steer head. There were shelves and shadowboxes containing statues of coyotes, a Hopi Indian playing the flute, a Saguaro cactus, and a road runner. Pottery sat on the end table opposite the commode, and a wall mounted magazine rack was filled with western travel guides.

If word gets out about the men's room, visitors may request conducted tours. "Why not add on a gift shop?" I thought. I have been to museums much less impressive than the men's room at Rustic Ranch Elementary School.

I spent my afternoon tutoring Bryson, a fourth grade student who had fallen behind in his math assignments. We selected one of his 12 unfinished worksheets and began. It called for the simple addition of two decimal numbers. Bryson had his own system of addition. Instead of starting with the rightmost column of numbers and working left, he started at the leftmost column and worked right. He invariably got the wrong answers. I repeatedly showed him the correct way, but he informed me that my way was wrong, his way was right, and that his answers were right. In his heart of hearts, he genuinely believed that he was right and that the accepted laws of mathematics were in error.

I was unable to get through to Bryson so I said, "Let's use a calculator to add these two numbers together, and maybe then you'll accept what I've been telling you." I made the calculation and showed him the correct answer. He sneered and told me that calculators were incapable of adding decimal numbers properly, and that only his system (in which 4 plus 2 equals 7) could be trusted to give the real answer.

The Sci-Fi movie "Journey to the Far Side of the Sun" starring Roy Thinnes was about an astronaut who made a trip around the sun, crash landed on what he thought was earth, and awoke to find that certain aspects of earth had changed. The people and places were the same, but communications and electronics were operating in ways that were foreign to his reality system. As it turned out, there was an alternate earth opposite our earth populated with Doppelgangers. Both planets were unaware that the other existed, and neither planet had ever seen the other, because the sun was always directly between them.

Was Bryson from a parallel world where F (force) did not equal M times A (mass times acceleration) and E (energy) was not equivalent to M C-squared (mass times the square of the speed of light)? He was either from an alternate world or he was the most stubborn and closed-minded little guy I have ever seen. In the comic strip BC, the character Wiley occasionally leans on a big rock, upon which are printed vocabulary words and their definitions. I can see the printing on the rock: "Mental Block" - See Bryson.

I spent at least two hours trying to coax Bryson to step into the real world. He chose to remain in his self-defined universe. In baseball terminology, this designated hitter had struck out with Bryson.

The last surprise of the day was an announcement by the principal that busses would be 30 minutes late. She informed teachers privately that there was a bomb threat at the school bus depot earlier in the day, thus the delay.

If I were editor of the Rustic Ranch Times, I would have had a choice of headlines that day:

"School Bus Bomb Threat"
"Western Museum Unveiled in Teachers Lounge"
"Laws of Mathematics Repealed at RR Elementary"

CHAPTER 45

Bubble Gum Bribe

Before becoming a substitute teacher, I worked 48 years as an aerospace engineer. Two-thirds of that time was spent in Houston, Texas at the Johnson Space Center with McDonnell Douglas (now Boeing) and Lockheed Martin.

I reported for duty at JSC during the summer of 1974. One of my earliest tasks was an on-site assignment to support the Mission Planning and Analysis Division (MPAD), which was located in Building 30. Being new kid on the block, my civil servant friends were eager to show me the new neighborhood. Tom took me on a tour of the third floor. The first stop was Marty's office. We stepped into a room overloaded with reports and memos, which were stacked at least 18 inches high on every horizontal surface, including the floor. MPAD personnel had dubbed Marty's office as the "eighth wonder of the aerospace world."

Twenty-five years later, I reported for duty at Rustic Ranch Elementary School. When I stepped into the fifth grade classroom, I had flashbacks of Marty's office. On the top of a stack of papers on the teacher's desk was an open math textbook and a clipboard containing the lesson plans. The math text was open to section 11.1 - "Decimal Quotients." From the lesson plans, I noticed that during math, which was the first subject of the day, we would focus on section 11.1. How lucky can you get?

During the math lesson, I wrote a principle of division on an old fashioned blackboard:

"When the divisor is greater than the dividend, the quotient will be a decimal and less than one."

After verifying that this was a new concept for them, I shared a saying that came from the book, "Quotable Quotes":

"Man's mind, once enlarged by a new idea, never returns to its original dimensions."

The class pondered these two statements and smiled. Audrey exclaimed (tongue-in-cheek): "Oh, my head is tingling and I can feel it getting larger!"

In the comic strip, "Peanuts," one of the characters - Pigpen - always walks around in a hazy cloud of dust - it's his trademark. One of the fifth graders - Brad - always had untied shoelaces flapping about his feet - it was his trademark. The first time I kneeled down to tie his shoes, Brad said, "My grandpa lives up in the mountains, and he has hair just like yours." I chuckled and replied, "It's called old hair." I gave the bow an extra knot to keep the laces in place. Twenty minutes later I noticed that Brad's laces were untied again.

During the Language Arts period, each child wrote a "fractured fairy tale" story. Obviously the regular teacher had been brought up on Bullwinkle TV cartoons. Most of the kids plagiarized familiar fairy tales. Audrey wrote about the three little hamburgers who were running from the big, bad cow. Pam wrote about a girl who lived in a high rise condo. She had mega-finger nails, which she hung out of her penthouse window, so her boyfriend "Nail File" could grab them and climb up to his lover. Larry had the most original story - "The Invisible Flying Fish Boy." Larry told me, "My story is about a boy who was hit by a meteorite and gained special powers. He was able to turn himself into an invisible flying fish." (I think he was inventing his story in real time.)

While the kids were outside having recess, I took my sack lunch to the teachers' lounge. Three teachers were already there eating macaroni and cheese, cooked in the school cafeteria. I couldn't resist saying, "I understand that school administrators have ordered cafeteria cooks to put sand in the macaroni and cheese." They gave me a startled look, gave their macaroni and cheese a suspicious look, and asked, "Why?" I replied, "To improve the traction." Nobody laughed at my inside joke - apparently the kids at this school kept the macaroni and cheese on their plates and off the floor.

As we consumed our lunch, loud banging sounds came from the far wall of the lounge. The three munchers of macaroni and cheese seemed oblivious to the sounds. I asked, "What is that pounding sound I hear?" The most senior teacher replied, "Oh, that's the towel dispenser in the boy's rest room - it's mounted on the other side of the wall." It was the common model that had a lever at the side. You push down on the lever and a six-inch section of towel comes out the bottom. If you want a twelve-inch section, you push the lever twice before tearing off the paper towel. "Thunk, thunk, tear" was the pattern. There was no let-up to the noise, and I wondered if a team of students had planned a conspiracy to ruin their teachers' lunch period by maintaining a relentless racket, using the towel dispenser as their weapon of choice.

When the fifth graders returned from recess, three of them hobbled in late, reminding me of Archibald Willard's famous Revolutionary War painting, "The Spirit of '76," which shows a young drummer boy, his elderly partner, and a bandaged fife player, marching proudly and resolutely across the battlefield. The three miniature fifth grade warriors were casualties of the daily soccer game. Elizabeth had a smashed nose, Jennifer had a sprained thumb, and Angelo had a head injury. I dispatched all three to the school nurse. The informal noon hour soccer games are not for the faint hearted!

At 3:30 P.M. the kids had already donned their jackets and backpacks and were lining up at the door. I noticed that the floor of the room looked like the quintessential carnival grounds at closing time. Remembering the psychology lesson I learned a year earlier from a fourth grader - "You've got to trick them" - I exclaimed, "Ugh! Look at the messy floor! I have a piece of bubble gum for anyone who places trash in the wastebasket." A mad scramble ensued. Kids clustered around the wastebasket, some holding mega-debris such as multiple sheets of notebook paper; others holding miniscule debris, such as the miniature flag from a Hershey's kiss. One and all got the promised reward, and the floor was immaculate. I checked the contents of the bulging wastebasket, and discovered that in their zeal, some had discarded their fractured fairy tales. (I added them to the growing stack of papers on the teacher's desk.)

President Dwight D. Eisenhower, in his autobiography "Stories I Tell My Friends," wrote about a visit to his uncle's farm. Eisenhower ("Ike") was only 5 years old at the time, and, as he tried to explore the farm, a hostile gander chased and terrorized him. Ike's uncle came to the rescue. He armed Ike with an old broom, shortened to make a perfect weapon for a barnyard explorer. When the gander attempted to nip Ike's behind, the little lad hauled off and whacked the gander in the tail feathers with the nubbin end of the broom. From them on, Ike was the boss of the barnyard. The President said he learned a valuable lesson that day - one which he remembered all his life: "Always negotiate with your adversary from a position of power." The lesson I have learned as a sub is: "Never underestimate the power of a bubble gum bribe."

After cleaning the room, the fifth graders once again lined up at the door praying for an early release. The clock still showed 3:30 P.M. The bell wouldn't sound until 3:45 P.M. Another Einstein time dilation. Knowing that they would not do a lick of work if I sat them back at their desks, I said, "Let's take an early release!" Their response was a roar of approval. We all headed for the playground, which was adjacent to the bus pick-up lanes. I overheard two boys talking when we reached the playground. One was telling the other, "We got bubble gum and an early release today. I wish our substitute would come back and be our regular teacher!" I didn't want to hear that. Substitutes should never be that good - our job is not to bury regular teachers, but to praise them.

My last benevolent act of the day was to pick a squashed banana (with the fingernails of my forefinger and thumb) from the playground sidewalk and to drop it into the trash barrel. The Neil Armstrong in me couldn't help but say, "That's one small step for safety; one giant leap for good housekeeping."

CHAPTER 46

Sanitized Ears

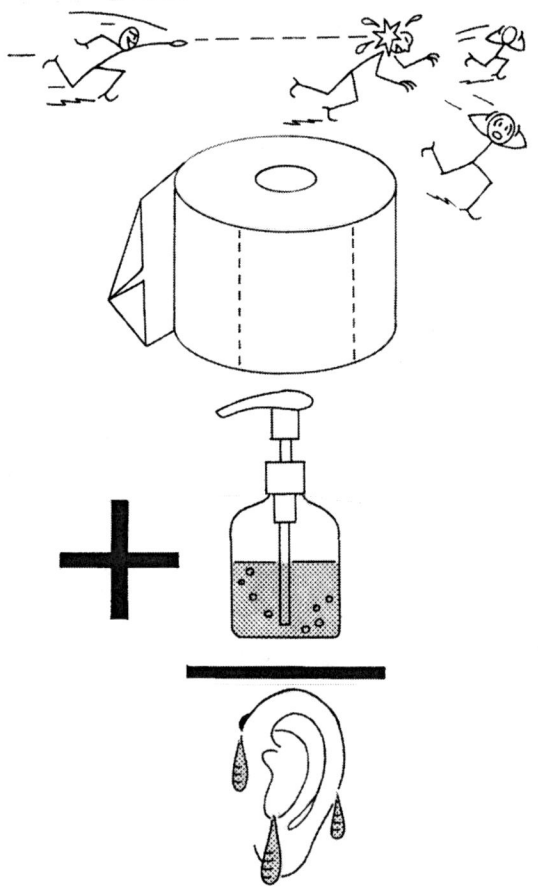

 March 4th I returned to Falcon Crest Middle School to substitute for Miss Krems, the Special Ed teacher. She was attending a math seminar that day. This was the school whose motto was "Safe, Responsible, Respectful." This was the school where pink apparel was verboten. This was also the school with the Marilyn Monroe photographs in the men's room.
 Miss Krems wasn't the only one studying math that day. The Special Ed kids had math during first period. They were to take a quiz over

perimeters, areas, and volumes. Prior to distributing the quizzes, I reviewed the basics of geometry by asking:

"What does 'perimeter' mean?" Samantha responded with "the distance around an object or shape." I continued, "What is 'area'?" Again, Samantha's hand shot up, and she replied, "the space inside a flat shape." "OK, define 'volume'." Samantha made a triple kill by stating (with great authority): "the space inside a three dimensional object."

I was really impressed, so I complimented her, "You must be a true genius, Samantha!" The entire class laughed. Then Arthur spoke, "Look behind you on the blackboard, Mr. K." I turned around and discovered that the teacher had written those definitions on the blackboard the previous day, and Samantha had merely read them off the board. Well, if not a genius, at least observant.

The next period, I accompanied four of my Special Ed kids to Social Studies. Mr. Hall was the teacher and the subject was Ancient Rome. The class had to write in their journals five chapter highlights, for example:

1. In 100 BC, wealthy Romans (including members of the Senate) bought up all the farm land and put small farmers out of business.
2. The poor flocked to the big cities, and politicians gained popularity by providing cheap food and entertainment for them.
3. Tiberius and Gaius Gracchus sought reforms and asked the Senate to transfer ownership of public lands back to the poor.
4. Many of the senators owned public land and placed their own interests above the general welfare of the people.
5. The unscrupulous senators had Tiberius killed in 133 BC and his brother Gaius killed twelve years later.

This historic situation and the lesson learned (buck the system and it will destroy you) reminded me of an episode from the Peanuts comic strip. Charlie Brown was talking to Lucy about the trouble he was having with the library over a lost book. She replied: "It has been my experience that when an individual takes on an institution, there is a tendency for the institution to win." Charlie Brown fell to the ground, stunned. Lucy asked, "What's the matter, Charlie Brown?" He replied, "The hearing of a great truth always stuns me!"

At lunchtime, I headed for the teachers' lounge. That morning the teachers' lounge had served as the math seminar room. The teachers who had been attending math training, including Miss Krems, were just leaving the room. I joined three other sixth grade teachers. They were chuckling over something. I discovered that one of the teachers had taken a cell phone from a student. Students are not allowed to use cell phones in class

- no talking or texting allowed. Miss Persimmons had not only confiscated the phone, but she was reading the student's text messages. Regarding the school motto, "Safe, Responsible, Respectful," something failed to add up in the math seminar room, a.k.a. the teachers' lounge!

Had cell phones and computers been available in George Washington's times, I am almost certain that he would have added another rule of civility and decent behavior: "If one finds in his possession information that is private and personal to another individual, he shall show respect for that individual by keeping that information confidential."

The last period of the day was Study Hall. If I've said it once, I've said it a dozen times - "Nothing good ever happens in Study Hall, a.k.a., Advisory Period, especially if it happens to be the last period of the day (and especially if it's Friday)."

Michael sauntered into the room spinning a basketball and looking like he made the cut for the Harlem Globetrotters. There was an umbrella on the desk in the back of the room. Recall that the umbrella is the weapon of choice for the Penguin, Batman's arch enemy. It turns out that the umbrella was also the weapon of choice for John. He grabbed the umbrella, flourished it above his head, and closed in on a fellow classmate. In the true spirit of Batman, I came to the rescue and returned the umbrella to its original resting place. Angelo, meanwhile, was trying out his latest Jujitsu moves on a skinny-armed student, and again I came to the rescue. Study Halls are a time for interventions by superheroes.

Having calmed the troops, I looked around for other nefarious activities. It didn't take long to spot one. Sitting on John's desk was a roll of toilet paper, and sitting alongside the roll was a plastic pump container of hand sanitizer. Normal human beings would use the toilet paper to clean up spills or to blow one's nose, not to mention the common bathroom application. Hand sanitizer would be used to clean one's hands after completing a craft or prior to going to the cafeteria.

But we were not dealing with normal humans here. John tore six tissues off the roll, soaked them in hand sanitizer, rolled the tissues into a ball the size of a marble, and threw it across the room, trying to lodge it in Michael's ear. Again, Batman to the rescue!

Joseph began the period searching for working markers. The set in the room were dried out. He was completing a geological chart. When the bell rang, he hadn't added a single letter to the chart. Kids left the room with hand sanitizer on their clothing, or dripping from their ears. All had smiles. All were as happy as if they had good sense.

CHAPTER 47

Author, Author

One of the hit tunes from Rogers and Hammerstein's musical, "The King and I," was "Getting to Know You." That's exactly what happens when you substitute in the same class two or more consecutive days. During my two-day "gig" at Rustic Ranch Elementary School, I got to know Mrs. Sanders' (in her own words) "Twenty-five wonderful fifth graders."

When I first stepped into Mrs. Sanders' room I noticed a half-dozen big plastic tubs, which she used to store student folders, worksheets, and other class projects. Each tub contained twenty-five custom dividers made of 1/8 inch Masonite. There was also a four-foot tall Masonite and pine book rack containing books, which the students had written that semester. Each book was 5-1/2 by 8-1/2 inches in size, had laminated covers, and was held together by a plastic spiral spine. It was hard to decide which accomplishment was more praiseworthy - the writing of the books or the construction of the Masonite and pine book rack.

Students weren't due to arrive for twenty minutes, so after I reviewed the lesson plans, I perused the bookshelf to see what the students had written. Here are some of the titles: The Evil Doctor, Super Chihuahua, The Banana Hunt, Funkatator Professor, The Robot Santa, The Day Hot Dogs Took Over the World, Attack of the Zombies, and Ant Wars. "What twisted minds," I thought. "My kind of people."

The kids arrived, and, after the usual attendance taking, lunch counting, and flag pledging, we launched into Math. Students completed their math worksheets in record time, proving that they were not only published authors, but that they also possessed wonderful computing skills. I was in the midst of twenty-five ambidextrous right-brain, left-brain superstars.

I looked at the schedule and saw that we had about twenty minutes to spend before Social Studies. Since each student had not only written his or her book, but had also illustrated it, I wondered if they might profit from a lesson in cartooning. When I asked them, "Would you like to learn how to draw cartoons?" I heard twenty-five enthusiastic yeses.

These fifth graders were the perfect apprentices. They learned how to draw the balloon head, stick figures, and Dick Tracy - one of my all time favorites. Throughout the day, students showed up at my desk requesting that I draw specific pictures for them. Some were for upcoming books, others were just for fun (or to test me). I drew: dogs, elephants, penguins, a WWII airplane, a storm trooper, Iron Man, an elk, the Steelers' logo, the Redskins' logo, a spider, a miniature Chihuahua, Tweety Bird, a soldier, and zombies.

Two boys had special requests. Edgar wanted me to draw him as a hobo, which I did. Brent wanted me to draw him as a Jedi warrior (with cape). Done. By the time these two boys reach ninth grade they will have matured and no doubt changed their career goals - perhaps to male stripper and demolitionist. If and when that happens, I will refuse to illustrate those two professions.

In social studies, students were presented a dilemma, once faced by early American settlers. Students pretended to be part of a wagon train heading west that got off to a late start. They reached Snow Pass in November. They had to make a tough decision, and list the pros and cons on a worksheet. The options were: 1) Press forward to claim the land, but risk being frozen in Snow Pass; 2) Return to the safety of their home town of Paradise and start again next spring; 3) Camp where they were and wait out the winter.

The only less-than-wonderful event of the day - something very unsocial - occurred in Social Studies. As students were turning in their Wagon Train decision worksheets, two modern day settlers got into a shoving match. Miss Mitchell, a teacher from an adjacent fifth grade classroom, happened to be passing our doorway at the time and beat me to the site of the scuffle. The two combatants spent recess in the Principal's office (and never reached Snow Pass).

Language Arts was the last class of the day. This was Author's Workshop Day, and students took turns sitting on a director's chair and reading their latest books to their twenty-four fellow authors. My job was to introduce each author, by reading the "About the Author" section of their books. Quite honestly, most ten year olds have a lackluster biography, and most of my introductions went like this: "Meet Marcie, who was born in Tucson, Arizona in 1998. Her favorite pet is her cat Missy, and her favorite food is pizza." Incidentally, all of them mentioned pizza in their biographies, indicating that they were ready for middle school, where pizza is king.

Brice, one of the wagon train combatants, wrote an unusual story. School regulations prohibit violence between humans, be it fact or fiction, so Brice wrote about violent confrontations between food groups. Pizzas were killing off rival hamburger gangs, macaroni and cheese dishes were mauling bowls of Jell-O, and so on. Some might consider Brice's story a little farfetched, but if the truth be told, I've eaten combinations of food that felt like they were at war in my stomach.

After about the third story, I noticed that little minds started to wander. Here are a few things fifth graders do when forced to listen to their classmates read a story in a barely audible, monotone voice: jab your finger with an open safety pin, play with a plastic slinky, roll dice, play "which hand" with the dice, pull the plastic spine off a neighbor's book, hum an aimless tune, disassemble a ball point pen, tear and wad up a piece of paper, punch the person next to you on the shoulder, and balance yourself on two chair legs.

Relief came when a student noticed that it was time to go to Music. Everyone, including me breathed a sigh of relief. The last three readers had been boys who formed an author's conspiracy. Chuck had read Penguin Club. Joe followed by reading Penguin Club II, and Brad put the final glaze on our eyes with Penguin Club III.

As the kids took to the halls in anticipation of the school busses, they joined other fifth graders. I heard whispering coming from the little clusters of humanity, and noticed that my class was showing the other students the cartoons I had drawn for them. Little heads turned in my direction with looks of great admiration. The halls were alive with exclamations of "Wow" and "Gee."

My twenty-five wonderful students turned into twenty-five wonderful press agents, and I felt like I was only about one bag of confetti shy of a ticker tape parade.

CHAPTER 48

Red Carpet Event

On a windy Thursday in March, I accepted an assignment to teach special education (Special Ed) kids at the Precious Solace elementary school. The good thing about a Special Ed assignment is, there are fewer octopuses in the classroom to slip socks onto. The bad news is, Special Ed kids wiggle the socks off faster. Class size was four. One was absent, so it was a three octopus day.

Miss Wendy was the teacher's aide. She and I met the kids at the drop-off area and then headed directly to the cafeteria for breakfast.

Jeremiah, Ned, and Dee Dee loaded their trays with sausage, biscuits and gravy, toast and jelly, and juice. They began the day with a solid "brownie breakfast." The latter term was coined by my second grade teacher at the Mt. Oliver Elementary School (MOES) in Pittsburgh. Since there was no cafeteria at MOES, we ate breakfast before coming to school. Every morning Miss Nibs asked each child what he or she ate for breakfast. If you happened to have a "brownie breakfast," namely, bacon, eggs, juice, cereal, milk, and toast, she pasted a gold star beside your name on the Brownie Breakfast Chart. (I only had one star that semester, and I must confess that I fibbed to Miss Nibs to get it.)

We left the cafeteria and headed for the classroom. Ned was wearing a coating of sausage bits and gravy on his cheeks and chin. The first "octopus sock" of the day was to wash Ned's face. After the kids put away their backpacks and coats, Miss Wendy and I escorted our three eight-year olds to the gym, because this happened to be "Picture Day."

When we arrived, there were between 50 and 100 children - first and second graders - lined up along the walls ready to have their pictures taken. Never have so many toothless grins gathered in one place. The kids in this school alone must have sent the tooth fairy into overtime, or forced her into early retirement. While we waited our turn, I asked Ned to practice his smile. He gave me the equivalent of a toothless grimace.

I've seen TV clips of the Hollywood stars arriving for Oscar night - dressed in their finest, and stopping on the red carpet to pose for photographers. There is also a new TV show about Tots in Tiaras. What we had on Picture Day was a combination of these two phenomena.

Little Miss Far-Out wore designer sunglasses, golden slippers, and a two-foot long hair extension consisting of wavy, fire-engine-red cords, which was clipped to her Afro-colored hair with a silver, star-shaped beret. Miss Cinderella wore a sheer, peach-colored, off-the-shoulder, mid-calf-length gown, peppered with glittering sequins. I was tempted to ask her to twirl and grant me a wish. Miss December wore a satin, yuletide-red, ankle-length skirt with a white fur collar. She also wore red high-heeled shoes. Miss Flapper had an off-the-shoulder, pink, above-the-knee length dress with pleated skirt, and wore a matching pink elastic hair band neatly containing her page-boy bob hairdo. It wouldn't have surprised me in the least if she were to do the Charleston dance on the gym floor, complete with palm-crossovers and coordinated knee knocking.

The lady in charge carried a plastic tub full of black plastic combs. She went up and down the lines of kids handing them out to the young ladies. She didn't bother giving the boys any. Lost cause. Some teachers helped the girls get their locks in place prior to the group pictures.

Jeremy wore a long-sleeved striped shirt that looked pretty sharp when we arrived. By the time it was his turn to sit before the camera, he had stretched it into a bell shape. He grinned, the camera clicked, and the rest was history.

On the way back to the classroom, Ned turned to Miss Wendy and I and said one of his four favorite sentences: "Go potty!" We stopped at the little boys room. (The other three were: "Go recess; Go lunch; and Go home.") Moments later, Ned gave me a hint that it was sock time in octopus land. He hopped out into the corridor stark naked from the belly button to the ankles. My job - help him pull up his shorts and jeans.

We finally got back to the classroom and "hit the books." Ned, in an apparent effort to make a good impression on the substitute teacher (me), really applied himself to the "learn the colors" and the "learn the alphabet" folders. After about 30 minutes, Miss Wendy interrupted us saying, "Come on Ned, it's time for recess!" Ned would not leave the table, which really amazed Miss Wendy. Later in the afternoon, the novelty of my presence had worn off.

Twenty minutes before the appointed time. Ned began repeating his "Go lunch" mantra.

Miss Wendy and I took the trio to lunch. When in Rome do as the Romans. I bought my lunch along with the kids. I had the sausage pizza, green beans, the lettuce and cucumber salad, the chocolate chip cookie, and the half-pint of chocolate milk. I purposely passed up the dinosaur pasta, which looked a lot like macaroni and cheese. Ned also had the sausage pizza.

There is an expression, "He wears his emotions on his sleeve." In Ned's case the expression is, "He wears his sausage on his cheeks and chin." When we got to the classroom, I again washed the sausage from Ned's kisser. But the damage had already been done. Ned had a permanent sausage ring around his mouth that no amount of scrubbing could remove.

The kids did a color by numbers worksheet after lunch. For a moment I thought it was a scribbling contest, but when I looked more closely, I was delighted to find that Jeremiah was a pretty decent artist. Unlike his two classmates, he had stayed between the lines and created a respectable, three-color picture of a rose.

Miss Wendy asked me to read the afternoon story, which was "My Lucky Day." To make a long story short, a dirty Piglet knocks at Fox's door. Fox says, "This is my lucky day - lunch has come to me!" Piglet hops out of the roasting pan and tricks Fox into giving him a bath (it is unsanitary to eat dirty food); preparing him a sumptuous dinner (why eat a skinny pig when you can eat a fat one?); and administering a massage (it is best to tenderize meat before cooking it). Fox fainted from exertion and the once dirty Piglet left with a bag of cookies, shouting, "This is my lucky day."

Ned picked up on the dirt part of the story and told me "I like dirt." He also added, "I like cookies." Dirt and cookies, pigs and boys - seen one you've seen them all! (We already knew that Ned liked sausage.)

I stepped to the whiteboard and showed Dee Dee, Jeremiah, and Ned how to draw Piglet, Fox, and cookies. Dee Dee and Jeremiah were copying those drawings. Ned wandered around the room. After a brief stop to draw a cookie, Ned joined me at the whiteboard and erased the pictures I had drawn. This drew boos from Miss Wendy. Ned reminded me of the dog with the whisk-broom head in Disney's "Alice in Wonderland," who erased the trail Alice was following.

Just before afternoon recess, we lost Jeremiah, the "King of Crayons." He may have been able to contain the movement of his crayons, but he was unable to contain the movement of his bowels. We witnessed an unpleasant overflow from shorts and jeans. Miss Wendy escorted him to the office, and the school secretary summoned his Mom to pick him up.

At afternoon recess, Dee Dee had a number 1 accident. Luckily Dee Dee's mom had provided an extra set of jeans in her backpack and Miss Wendy came to the rescue and helped Dee Dee into her new (dry) wardrobe.

Dee Dee and Ned spent the remainder of the day pecking away at "Mighty Moe." Mighty Moe is a touch screen, audio visual device that helps Special Ed kids develop their vocabularies. There are pictures on the screen - of people, objects, and sentences. When you touch a picture on the screen, Mighty Moe pronounces the words. Dee Dee and Ned alternated between "Go Potty" and "Go Recess." The words rang through the room repeatedly like a perpetual echo. Finally I said, "Enough!" I washed their greasy finger prints off the screen, switched off Mighty Moe, and asked them to put on their coats and backpacks. When I turned to help Dee Dee with her coat, Ned switched Mighty Moe back on and resumed pressing the "Go Potty, Go Recess" buttons. I switched it off again and turned to help Ned get into his coat and backpack. Dee Dee promptly switched Mighty Moe back on and the cycle continued. Perfect example of putting socks on an octopus. Mighty Moe and I were thankful that all four regulars weren't present that day.

CHAPTER 49

Movin' and Groovin'

The school secretary of Colonel Dexter North Elementary (CDNE) called me in mid March and asked me to substitute for Miss Thistle, their music teacher. She said, "I understand that you have a musical background." I exclaimed, "I'm your man!" On Monday morning, I slipped my musical bang-clank equipment into my Texas brief case, donned my Kid Shelleen black outfit, grabbed my trumpet, and headed for CDNE.

Miss Thistle teaches music to about 850 elementary children, but not all at once. She schedules five to six classes per day, Kindergarten through fifth grades. Each class is on a two week cycle. During my two days, I taught ten classes.

Since I had musical experience, Miss Thistle didn't water down the assignments. She allowed me to follow her normal routine. I walked into a double portable building, found her lesson plans, and prepared to step into her world. She had established a ritual, and I tried to follow it to a tee. My first order of business, before the kids arrived, was to learn how to operate an MP3. Every single grandchild in the universe can do this. I had to follow the step-by-step procedures Miss Thistle had kindly prepared. I was an MP3 neophyte.

The Kindergarten kids arrived at 8:35 A.M. They sat in a circle on the floor. I gave them my widest musical smile, introduced myself as Mr. K, and distributed their name tag badges. Miss Thistle said I was to sing their name using "sol-mi," which happens to be the first two notes of the National Anthem. After they sang their two-note reply, "I'm here" (also sol-mi), I was to pitch their badge to them. It was like pitching cards into a hat, only in this case, the hats had little arms. By the end of the day, my tosses across the room to the little flinching fingers were gaining speed and accuracy and were drawing applause.

The next item in the daily routine was called Movin' and Groovin'. I turned on the MP3, pretending to be an MP3 expert, and called on a girl to be the leader. I watched as she extemporaneously created an on-the-spot dance to fit the music. The rest of the class had to imitate her moves. After 20 seconds, I slapped a tall drum, which signaled her to pick a boy to be the next leader. The boy made his moves, and so on. We repeated this cycle until the song ended.

Miss Thistle opens all her classes (K through 5th) with these two activities, namely the singing badge toss and the interpretive dance routine. The fourth and fifth graders had developed some pretty sophisticated dance moves for their Movin' and Groovin' sessions. One wiry girl did a vertical leap and twisted 360 degrees in the air before landing. Few if any of her classmates could duplicate that move! A boy tried a dance move that I called, "The Spastic Stork." He clutched one leg to his torso, hopped, jumped, and spun on the other leg, then collapsed to the floor. A few other boys came close to duplicating the moves. The girls froze, crossed their arms, and looked upon the exhibition with utter disgust!

For the kindergartners, I read them a book about a grouchy lady bug who declared war on the animal kingdom. During the story, I stopped and asked the kids to provide animal sound effects using triangles, ratchets, cymbals, gongs, wind chimes, tambourines, step bells, and other fascinating rhythm instruments. We heard from fireflies, a yellow-jacket, a stag beetle, a praying mantis, and on up the animal chain to an elephant and a whale. Near the end of the story, the little kindergartners had forgotten which animal they had been assigned (so did I), so I just pointed to one of them and smiled when I needed an animal sound.

The first grade class came in at 9:30 A.M., and after the badge tossing and Movin' and Groovin,' I passed along Miss Thistle's compliments to the class for their performance at the previous week's concert. She had prepared a two-part reward for the first graders. Part one was the privilege of watching a Bugs Bunny cartoon on TV.

I suppose Miss Thistle could justify this as a legitimate educational experience, because the soundtrack featured: Rossini's Barber of Seville; portions of the William Tell Overture; and excerpts from Wagnerian operas. It starred the classic Warner Brothers cartoon icons like Bugs Bunny, Elmer Fudd, Daffy Duck, Sylvester Pussycat, and Yosemite Sam.

As an aside, I used to practice my trumpet in the early morning before going to my engineering job. My little grandson Matthew had spent the night on this particular occasion. While I was practicing, Matthew wandered into my bedroom, spied a baton in my trumpet case, pulled it out, and began directing me. Out of the corner of my eye, I noticed that he was doing a remarkable job! I stopped playing, looked intently at him and asked, "Where did a little five-year-old like you learn to conduct music?" Without even blinking an eye he said, "I learned by watching Bugs Bunny cartoons." Who says cartoons are mindless wastes of time? (Not me.)

Part two of the first graders' reward was a peppermint candy cane. They were allowed to eat their treats during the movie. As Elmer Fudd and Bugs Bunny were twirling their batons before the Hollywood Bowl musicians, members of the audience were sucking the stems of their candy canes to fine points and jabbing one another with them. It reminded me of a scene from a prison movie, where convicts had fashioned simple objects - toothbrushes, spoons, etc. - into deadly weapons.

By the way, I had trouble loading the Bugs Bunny VCR tape into the player. It kept rejecting the tape. A little bespectacled boy came up to me and said, "May I help you? I know a lot about VCR's." I believed him. I said, "Go ahead." He gently grasped the tape with both hands, little pinkies pointed upward, and slid it in, saying, "You can't just jam the tape in - you must hold it like so and allow the machine to pull it in."

This reminded me of a scene from a Warner Brothers cartoon wherein the loquacious rooster, Foghorn Leghorn had been baffled by a barnyard problem and the brainy little chick with the thick lensed glasses came to his rescue. Brainy chick showed Foghorn the solution, backing it up with the appropriate diagrams and algebraic equations, which were neatly printed on his note pad. Sadly, I identified with Foghorn Leghorn.

The fourth graders were learning the names of the states and their capitols, in preparation for a future concert in which they would perform two snappy songs, namely, "Rap of the States" and "50 Nifty United States." I distributed 50 blue cards containing the names of the states and 50 yellow cards containing the names of the capitol cities. The kids had to circulate around the room, find the correct matches, and place the matched pair on the floor.

This proved to be a challenge, because most of the kids had not yet memorized states and capitols. They came to me with the hard questions, and I wasn't much help. (I did know that the capitol of Ohio was Columbus.) Luckily one of the fourth graders came to the rescue. He had a 3 by 10 inch piece of paper containing all 50 states and their capitols. It was rolled up into a scroll and wedged between his glasses and his nose.

In biblical times, religious men, especially the sect known as the Pharisees, used to wear "phylacteries" on their foreheads. The phylacteries contained laws and guidelines that the Pharisee would whip out when he needed to confront a sinner or to merely refresh his memory. Our personal fourth-grade phylactery bearer informed us that Boise was the capitol of Idaho, Concord was the capitol of New Hampshire, and so forth.

We wrapped up the class by singing a few refrains of the Rap of the States song. Then I lined them up, grabbed my trumpet, and marched them out the door and off into the sunset to the tune of "76 Trombones."

Chapter 50

Skunk Attack

My assignment to substitute for the music teacher at Colonel Dexter North Elementary lasted two days. The second day happened to be St. Patrick's Day and all the kids were dressed in green. Little girls wore green blouses, had green bows in their hair, and had green shamrock stickers pasted to their cheeks. The boys were also trimmed in green. One lad, no doubt a real Irishman, wore a green, Mardi-Gras, beaded chain with a green plastic shot glass dangling from it. I checked him to make sure he hadn't smuggled any Irish whiskey onto campus.

The kindergartners noticed that I was not wearing green. One sly little boy informed me that the penalty for not wearing green was that you got pinched. Twenty-three pairs of little eyes started to sparkle; twenty-three pairs of itchy little fingers began to twitch. In the nick-of-time, another little boy shouted "Stop! Mr. K has a green dot on his badge." I was saved! Actually, the dot was blue. Thank heavens for the occasional color blind kid coming to the rescue!

St. Patrick's Day was a day of commotion (and noise). We had a fire drill at 9:00 A.M., and I escorted the twenty-three kindergarten kids to the athletic field, where we lined up and waited for the all clear. In an adjacent field, some community bigwigs were filling a giant, multi-colored hot air balloon in preparation for a St. Patrick's Day ascent. Meanwhile, back at the music room, a skunk had crawled under Miss Thistle's music building, leaving an odor that everyone but me could smell when we got back. (I lost my sense of smell in Tucson, Arizona thirty-five years ago.)

On both days I saved the last ten minutes of each class for my "Timmy trumpet demonstration." I began by giving the kids a technical explanation of how pressing down one of the three valves caused air to detour through the associated section of pipe, thereby lengthening the instrument and producing a lower tone. It turns out, they weren't interested in plumbing details - they just wanted to hear me play a tune.

I asked them to lie on the floor, close their eyes, and pretend to be asleep. I said, "You are in a branch of the military service, you are sound asleep, and you are having pleasant dreams. Every morning the company bugler plays a song to tell you that it's time to rise and shine. It sounds like this." (I played Reveille, using an "inside" volume level).

They all jumped up to attention, smiled, and saluted me. I told them, "I played it rather softly for you. An actual military bugler would have played it much louder." They all shouted in unison, "We want to hear it louder!" I obliged them and won their little hearts.

Scientific principles are discovered by induction, whereby generalized conclusions are inferred from particular instances. Based on the fact that every class wanted to "hear it louder," I was ready to formulate a new "Great Truth," namely: "Kids crave cacophony, favor the fortissimo, and delight in decibels." But I wasn't the only noisemaker in the music room that St. Patrick's Day. The fifth graders would have their say.

As a prelude to the fifth grade's contribution to a noisy universe, I'd like to tiptoe into the past for an early childhood memory. My parents were members of a fraternal organization whose sole purpose was, as I understood it, partying. On New Year's Eve, members held a gala celebration with hats, noisemakers, and liquid refreshments. When the clock counted down to midnight, Dad, Mom, and their friends made quite a commotion with their noisemakers for about 60 seconds. Then they retired the noisemakers and returned to quieter forms of celebration. My brother and I inherited the noisemakers on January 1st (and performed a noisemaker encore at 8:00 A.M., which invariably annoyed our sleeping parents).

Back to the fifth grade story. Their assignment was to compose a three part song for rhythm instruments. The teacher had prepared the blank manuscripts and had prescribed that each song would be sixteen measures long. In a perfect world, each little composer would sit quietly, pen in hand, thoughtfully planning melodies, after-beats, and bass lines. Once the notes had been applied to paper, each fifth grader would assign the rhythm parts to three classmates and cautiously try out the finished composition.

Here is the real-world version of the fifth grade composition class at Colonel Dexter North Elementary. Most of the manuscripts ended up on the floor. Some had notes on them. About three students had actually followed directions and finished the assignment. The other twenty kids grabbed the noisiest rhythm instruments they could find, and, for the next fifty minutes produced a continuous string of white noise that would have been, if terminated after 60 seconds, the envy of every fraternal organization on New Year's Eve!

I stayed late to prepare the next day's name tags for Miss Thistle. As I sat at the desk, absorbed with my "paperwork," two cleaning ladies came through the door with brooms and vacuums. They wrinkled their noses and screeched in unison: "EEEE-OOOO-EEEE!" They turned to me and asked, "Don't you smell it?" "Huh?" I replied. "The skunk, the skunk!" they exclaimed.

I was aware that people with normal noses had smelled the skunk outside the portable earlier in the day, but I was unaware that the skunk was getting close and personal. Perhaps she had a nest under the portable. Perhaps the extra loud bugle calls (or the fifth grade composition class) had roused her pups and perturbed her to red-eyed fury. Perhaps she was chewing through the floor to wreak revenge on me! I grabbed my trumpet and made a hasty exit.

After dropping off the key and substitute folder at the office, I headed toward the parking lot. About six students, playing in an enclosed area spied me from the top of the sliding board. They shouted, "Hey, Mr. K, how about getting your trumpet out and playing us one last song before you go home?" I replied, "Sorry kids. I can't put you at risk for a skunk attack!"

ABOUT THE AUTHOR

Tim Kreiter has had the privilege of working 48 years as an aerospace engineer in support of various NASA programs. He retired in 2007 and chose to become a substitute teacher. "Adventures of a Substitute Teacher" is Tim's first book. Tim and his wife live in Rio Rancho, NM. His hobbies are cartooning, playing the trumpet, singing, collecting rocks, and reading. Tim continues to teach and is currently writing his second book, "More Adventures of a Substitute Teacher."

Recent Releases From Casa de Snapdragon

Visit http://www.casadesnapdragon.com for more information on these and many other books

They don't make memories like that anymore …
Katrina K Guarascio
ISBN: 978-1937240004
$13.95

Katrina Guarascio's collection "They Don't Make Memories…" explores the "slap and kick" of love, memory and destiny. These lyrical poems travel the complex and passionate journey between the "I" and "you,"--evoking the self, lover, friend, family member as well as river, flower, ocean and cloud. In these poems, the poet-speaker looks for and finds herself in the interweaving world. These poems embrace a large and personal universe that vibrates "between skin and bone," reverberating with song.

A Thousand Doors
Matt Pasca
ISBN: 978-0-9845681-6-1
$13.95

Poet Matt Pasca explores how personal suffering can be transformed into grace, as if through alchemy, when that grief can be shared with others. Using the Buddhist "Mustard Seed" parable as scaffolding, Pasca's work pays homage to Kisa Gotami's quest to save her son by finding a home where, impossibly, no suffering has befallen the inhabitants. Pasca's poems maneuver deftly between the seemingly simple and mundane details of the world around us and the sublime world we often miss in the myopia of our pain. Just as Gotami comes to see her grief reflected in the eyes behind the doors upon which she desperately knocks, we too find our own sorrows and pleasures illumined by the light of Pasca's unflinching exploration and delicate crafting. In the end, A Thousand Doors testifies to the necessity of sharing our stories with courage and vulnerability, and how doing so can lead us further down the path of joy.

In the Language of Women
Charles Adès Fishman
ISBN: 978-0-9845681-5-4
$15.95

In his second book from Casa de Snapdragon, Charles Adès Fishman focuses entirely on women - their memories, dreams, griefs, triumphs, and visions. In the Language of Women honors women's lives and frees the voices of those who have found it difficult, if not impossible, to address actions and events that have wounded and transformed them. It is also a book of fifty-two unforgettable poems in which the distinctive journeys of more than thirty women have been rescued from oblivion and brought to vivid life.

Dark Salt: A Brush with Genius
Lynn Strongin
ISBN: 978-0-9845681-4-7
$15.95

In this collection of late works by Lynn Strongin, we find that perfect balance of salt and water spiced with symbolism and metaphor that poet Strongin does so well. Jewish Temple offerings included salt and Jewish people still dip their bread in salt on the Sabbath as a remembrance of those sacrifices.

Silverton Gold
Jon Hovis
ISBN: 978-0-9845681-0-9
$13.95

From the author of "Preacher" and "The Feather Gang" comes an historically accurate tale of a Pinkerton agent tracking stolen gold and outlaws in the high country of Colorado. This wonderful novel showcases life, danger, and mining in the wild west of the 1890s.

Harriet Murphy: A Little Bit of Something
Janet K Brennan
ISBN: 978-0-9793075-6-0
$15.95

Come in, enjoy a cup of coffee, and sit a spell with Harriet Murphy as she regales you with her tales of family, life, and love in the early 1900's in the former gold mining town of Old Pine near Lake Tahoe in Northern California. Her tales revolve around a woman living alone in the hills of the Sierra Nevada with her horse, Pager, and a myriad of other wonderful and colorful characters. Her humble abode is the log cabin that her father built for her family soon after he came across the country in the great gold rush of 1849. Although he never struck it rich in the mines, he found it a unique, yet ideal, place to live and care for his wife and daughter, Henrietta.

CPSIA information can be obtained
at www.ICGtesting.com
Printed in the USA
FSOW02n0950080117
29383FS